Blazor Revealed

Building Web Applications in .NET

Peter Himschoot

Apress®

Blazor Revealed: Building Web Applications in .NET

Peter Himschoot
Melle, Belgium

ISBN-13 (pbk): 978-1-4842-4342-8
https://doi.org/10.1007/978-1-4842-4343-5

ISBN-13 (electronic): 978-1-4842-4343-5

Library of Congress Control Number: 2019932722

Managing Director, Apress Media LLC: Welmoed Spahr
Acquisitions Editor: Jonathan Gennick
Development Editor: Laura Berendson
Coordinating Editor: Jill Balzano

Cover designed by eStudioCalamar

Cover image designed by Freepik (www.freepik.com)

Distributed to the book trade worldwide by Springer Science+Business Media New York, 233 Spring Street, 6th Floor, New York, NY 10013. Phone 1-800-SPRINGER, fax (201) 348-4505, e-mail orders-ny@springer-sbm.com, or visit www.springeronline.com. Apress Media, LLC is a California LLC and the sole member (owner) is Springer Science + Business Media Finance Inc (SSBM Finance Inc). SSBM Finance Inc is a **Delaware** corporation.

For information on translations, please e-mail rights@apress.com, or visit www.apress.com/rights-permissions.

Apress titles may be purchased in bulk for academic, corporate, or promotional use. eBook versions and licenses are also available for most titles. For more information, reference our Print and eBook Bulk Sales web page at www.apress.com/bulk-sales.

Any source code or other supplementary material referenced by the author in this book is available to readers on GitHub via the book's product page, located at www.apress.com/9781484243428. For more detailed information, please visit www.apress.com/source-code.

Table of Contents

About the Author

 **Peter Himschoot** works as a lead trainer, architect, and strategist at U2U Training. Peter has a wide interest in software development, which includes applications for the Web, Windows, and mobile devices. Peter has trained thousands of developers, is a regular speaker at international conferences, and has been involved in many web and mobile development projects as a software architect. Peter is also a Microsoft Regional Director, a group of trusted advisors to the developer and IT professional audiences, and to Microsoft.

About the Technical Reviewer

Gerald Versluis is a developer and Microsoft MVP from Holland with years of experience working with Xamarin, Azure, ASP.NET, and other .NET technologies. He has been involved in numerous projects, in various roles. A great number of his projects are Xamarin apps. Not only does Gerald like to code, but he is keen on spreading his knowledge as well as gaining some in the bargain. He speaks, provides training sessions, and writes blogs and articles in his spare time.

Acknowledgments

When Jonathan Gennick from Apress asked me if I would be interested in writing a book on Blazor, I felt honored and of course I agreed that Blazor deserves a book. Writing a book is a group effort, so I thank Jonathan Gennick and Jill Balzano for giving me tips on styling and writing this book, and I thank Gerald Versluis for doing the technical review and pointing out sections that needed a bit more explaining. I also thank Magda Thielman and Lieven Iliano from U2U Training, my employer, for encouraging me to write this book.

I thoroughly enjoyed writing this book and I hope you will enjoy reading and learning from it.

Introduction to WebAssembly and Blazor

I was attending the *Microsoft Most Valued Professional and Regional Directors Summit* when we were introduced to Blazor for the first time by *Steve Sanderson* and *Daniel Roth*. And I must admit I was super excited about Blazor! Blazor is a framework that allows you to build single-page applications (SPAs) using C# and allows you to run any standard .NET library in the browser. Before Blazor, your options for building a SPA were JavaScript or one of the other higher-level languages like TypeScript, which get compiled into JavaScript anyway. In this introduction, I will look at how browsers are now capable of running .NET assemblies in the browser using WebAssembly, Mono, and Blazor.

Blazor is, at the time of writing, an EXPERIMENTAL framework. I hope by the time you are reading this book that it has been made official by Microsoft.

A Tale of Two Wars

Think about it. The browser is one of the primary applications on your computer. You use it every day. Companies who build browsers know this very well and are bidding for you to use their browser. In the beginning of mainstream Internet, everyone was using *Netscape*. Microsoft wanted a share of the market, so in 1995 it built *Internet Explorer 1.0*, released as part of Windows 95 Plus! pack. Newer versions were released rapidly, and browsers started to add new features such as <blink> and <marquee> elements. This was the beginning of the first browser war, giving people (especially designers) headaches because some developers were building pages with blinking marque controls ☺. But developers were also getting sore heads because of incompatibilities between browsers. *The first browser war was about having more HTML capabilities than the competition.*

But all of this is now behind us with the introduction of HTML5 and modern browsers like Google Chrome, Microsoft Edge, Firefox, and Opera. HTML5 not only defines a series of standard HTML elements but also rules on how they should render, making it a lot easier to build a web site that looks the same in all modern browsers.

But let's go back to 1995, when *Brendan Eich* wrote a little programming language known as *JavaScript* (initially called *LiveScript*) in 10 days (What!?). It was called JavaScript because its syntax was very similar to Java.

JavaScript and Java are not related. Java and JavaScript have as much in common as ham and hamster (I don't know who formulated this first, but I love this phrasing).

Little did Mr. Eich know how this language would impact the modern Web and even desktop application development. In 1995, *Jesse James Garett* wrote a white paper called *Ajax (Asynchronous JavaScript and XML)*, describing a set of technologies where JavaScript is used to load data from the server and that data is used to update the browser's HTML, thus avoiding full page reloads and allowing for client-side web applications (applications written in JavaScript that run completely in the browser). One of the first companies to apply Ajax was Microsoft, when it built *Outlook Web Access (OWA)*. OWA is a web application almost identical to the Outlook desktop application but providing the power of Ajax. Soon other Ajax applications started to appear, with Google Maps stuck in my memory as one of the other keystone applications. Google Maps would download maps asynchronously, and with some simple mouse interactions allowed you to zoom and pan the map. Before Google Maps, the server would do the map rendering and a browser would display the map like any other image by downloading a bitmap from a server.

Building an Ajax web site was a major undertaking, which only big companies like Microsoft and Google could afford. This soon changed with the introduction of JavaScript libraries like jQuery and knockout.js. Today we can build rich web apps with Angular, React, and Vue.js. All of them use JavaScript or higher-level languages like TypeScript, which get complied into JavaScript. Which brings us back to JavaScript and the second browser war. JavaScript performance is paramount in modern browsers. Chrome, Edge, Firefox, and Safari are all competing with one another, trying to convince users that their browser is the fastest, with cool sounding names for their JavaScript engine like *V8* and *Chakra*. These engines use the latest optimization tricks like Just-in-Time (JIT) compilation where JavaScript gets converted into native code, as illustrated by Figure 1.

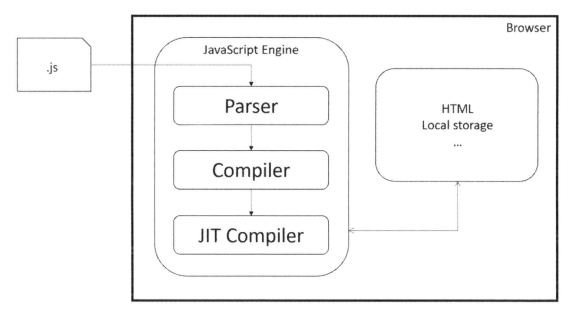

Figure 1. *The JavaScript execution process*

This process takes a lot of effort because JavaScript needs to be downloaded into the browser, where it gets parsed, then compiled into bytecode, and then JIT converted into native code. So how can we make this process even faster?

The second browser war is all about JavaScript performance.

Introducing WebAssembly

WebAssembly allows you to take the parsing and compiling to the server. With WebAssembly you compile your code in a format called WASM (an abbreviation of WebASseMbly), which gets downloaded by the browser where it gets JIT compiled into native code, as shown in Figure 2. Open your browser and google *"webassembly demo zen garden."* One of the links is `https://s3.amazonaws.com/mozilla-games/ZenGarden/EpicZenGarden.html` where you can see an impressive ray-trace demo of a Japanese Zen garden, shown in Figure 3.

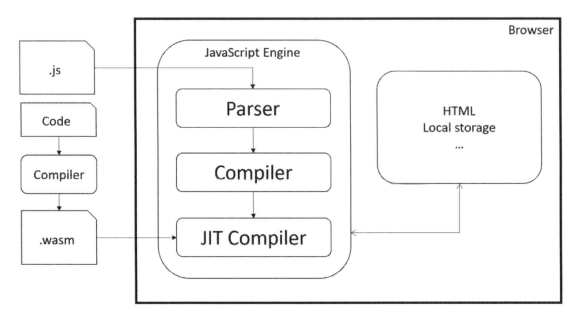

Figure 2. *The WebAssembly execution process*

Figure 3. *Japanese Zen Garden*

From the official site, `www.webassembly.org`:

WebAssembly (abbreviated Wasm) is a binary instruction format for a stack-based virtual machine. Wasm is designed as a portable target for compilation of high-level languages like C/C++/Rust, enabling deployment on the web for client and server applications.

So WebAssembly is a new binary format optimized for browser execution; it is NOT JavaScript. There are compilers for languages like C++ and Rust that compile to WASM.

Which Browsers Support WebAssembly?

WebAssembly is supported by all major browsers: Chrome, Edge, Safari, and Firefox, including their mobile versions. As WebAssembly becomes more and more important, we will see other modern browsers follow suit, but don't expect Internet Explorer to support WASM.

WebAssembly and Mono

Mono is an open source implementation of the .NET CLI specification, meaning that Mono is a platform for running .NET assemblies. Mono is used in *Xamarin* for building mobile applications that run on the Windows, Android, and iOS mobile operating systems. Mono also allows you to run .NET on Linux (its original purpose) and is written in C++. This last part is important because you saw that you can compile C++ to WebAssembly. So, what happened is that the Mono team decided to try to compile Mono to WebAssembly, which they did successfully. There are two approaches. One is where you take your .NET code and you compile it together with the Mono runtime into one big WASM application. However, this approach takes a lot of time because you need to take several steps to compile everything into WASM, which is not so practical for day-to-day development. The other approach takes the Mono runtime, compiles it into WASM, and this runs in the browser where it will execute .NET Intermediate Language just like normal .NET does. The big advantage is that you can simply run .NET assemblies without having to compile them first into WASM. This is the approach currently taken by Blazor. But Blazor is not the only one taking this approach. For example, the *Ooui* project allows you to run *Xamarin.Forms* applications in the browser. The disadvantage of this is that it needs to download a lot of .NET assemblies. This can be solved by using *Tree Shaking* algorithms, which remove all unused code from assemblies. These tools are not yet available, but they are in the pipeline.

Interacting with the Browser with Blazor

WebAssembly with Mono allows you to run .NET code in the browser. *Steve Sanderson* used this to build Blazor. Blazor uses the popular ASP.NET MVC approach for building applications that run in the browser. With Blazor, you build Razor files (Blazor = Browser + Razor) that execute inside the browser to dynamically build a web page. With Blazor, you don't need JavaScript to build a web app, which is good news for thousands of .NET developers who want to continue using C# (or F#).

How Does It Work?

Let's start with a simple Razor file. See Listing 1, which you can find when you create a new Blazor project.

Listing 1. The Counter Razor File

```
@page "/counter"

<h1>Counter</h1>

<p>Current count: @currentCount</p>

<button class="btn btn-primary" onclick="@IncrementCount">Click me</button>

@functions {
    int currentCount = 0;

    void IncrementCount()
    {
        currentCount++;
    }
}
```

This file gets compiled into .NET code (you'll find out how later in this book), which is then executed by the Blazor engine. The result of this execution is a tree-like structure called the *render tree*. The render tree is then sent to JavaScript, which updates the DOM to reflect the render tree (creating, updating, and removing HTML elements and attributes). Listing 1 will result in h1, p (with the value of currentCount) and button HTML elements. When you interact with the page, for example when you click the button, this will trigger the button's click event, which will invoke the `IncrementCount` method from Listing 1. The render tree is then regenerated, and any changes are sent again to JavaScript, which will update the DOM. This process is illustrated in Figure 4.

This model is very flexible. It allows you to build *progressive web apps*, and also can be embedded in *Electron* desktop applications, of which Visual Studio Code is a prime example.

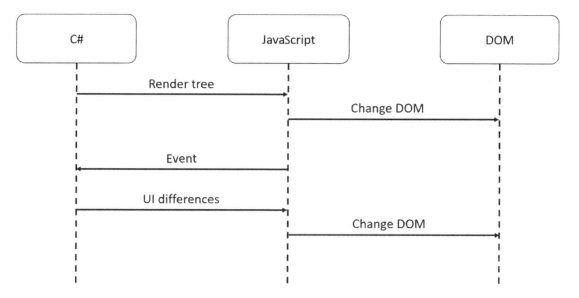

Figure 4. *The Blazor DOM generation process*

Server-Side Blazor

On August 7, 2018, Daniel Roth introduced a new execution model for Blazor called server-side Blazor at the *ASP.NET community standup*. In this model, your Blazor site runs on the server, resulting in a much smaller download for the browser.

The Server-Side Model

You just saw that client-side Blazor builds a *render tree* using the Mono runtime, which then gets sent to JavaScript to update the DOM. With server-side Blazor, the render tree gets built on the server and then gets serialized to the browser using *SignalR*. JavaScript in the browser then deserializes the render tree to update the DOM, which is pretty similar to the client-side Blazor model. When you interact with the site, events get serialized back to the server, which then executes the .NET code, updating the render tree, which then gets serialized back to the browser. You can see this process in Figure 5. The big difference is that there is no need to send the Mono runtime and your Blazor assemblies to the browser. And the programming model stays the same!

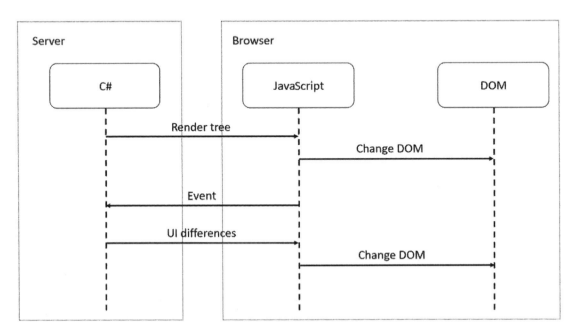

Figure 5. *Server-side Blazor*

Pros and Cons of the Server-Side Model

The server-side model has a couple of benefits, but also some drawbacks. Let's discuss them here so you can decide which model fits your application's needs.

Smaller Downloads

With server-side Blazor, your application does not need to download mono.wasm nor all your .NET assemblies. This means that the application will start a lot faster.

Development Process

Blazor client-side has limited debugging capabilities, resulting in added logging. Because your .NET code is running on the server, you can use the regular .NET debugger. You could start building your Blazor application using the server-side model and when it's finished switch to the client-side model by making a small change to your code.

.NET APIs

Because you are running your .NET code on the server you can use all the .NET APIs you would use with regular MVC applications, for example accessing the database directly. Note that doing this will stop you from being able to quickly convert it to a client-side application.

Online Only

Running the Blazor application on the server does mean that your users will always need access to the server. This will prevent the application from running in Electron; you also can't run it as a progressive web application (PWA). And if the connection drops between the browser and server, your user could lose some work because the application will stop functioning.

Server Scalability

All your .NET code runs on the server so if you have thousands of clients, your server(s) will have to handle all the work. Also, Blazor uses a state-full model, which means you must keep track of every user's state on the server.

Summary

In this introduction, you looked at the history of the browser wars and how they resulted in the creation of WebAssembly. Mono allows you to run .NET assemblies; because Mono can run on WebAssembly, you can now run .NET assemblies in the browser! All of this resulted in thc creation of Blazor, where you can build Razor files containing .NET code, which updates the browser's DOM, giving you the ability to build single-page applications in .NET.

CHAPTER 1

Your First Blazor Project

Getting a hands-on experience is the best way to learn. In this chapter, you'll install the prerequisites to developing with Blazor, which includes Visual Studio along with some needed extensions. Then you'll create your first Blazor project in Visual Studio, run the project to see it work, and inspect the different aspects of the project to get a "lay of the land" view for how Blazor applications are developed.

Installing Blazor Prerequisites

Working with Blazor requires you to install some prerequisites, so let's get to it.

.NET Core

Blazor runs on top of .NET Core, providing the web server for your project, which will serve the client files that run in the browser and run any server-side APIs that your Blazor project needs. .NET Core is Microsoft's cross-platform solution for working with .NET on Windows, Linux, and OSX.

You can find the installation files at www.microsoft.com/net/download. Look for the latest version of the .NET Core SDK. Download the installer, run it, and accept the defaults.

Verify the installation when the installer is done by opening a new command prompt and typing the following command:

```
dotnet –version
```

Look for the following output to indicate that you have the correct version installed. The version number should be at least 2.1.300.

Should the command's output show an older version (for example 2.1.200), you must download and install a more recent version of .NET Core SDK.

© Peter Himschoot 2019
P. Himschoot, *Blazor Revealed*, https://doi.org/10.1007/978-1-4842-4343-5_1

Visual Studio 2017

Visual Studio 2017 (from now on I will refer to Visual Studio as VS) is one of the integrated development environments (IDEs) you will use throughout this book. The other IDE is Visual Studio Code. With either one you can edit your code, compile it, and run it all from the same application. The code samples are also the same. However, VS only runs on Windows, so if you're using another OS, please continue to the section on Visual Studio Code.

Download the latest version of Visual Studio 2017 from `www.visualstudio.com/downloads/`.

Run the installer and make sure that you install the ASP.NET and web development role, as shown in Figure 1-1.

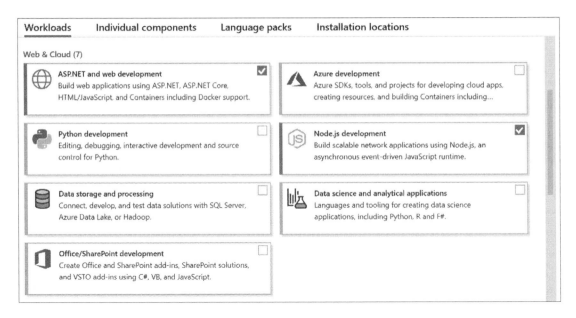

Figure 1-1. *The Visual Studio Installer Workloads selection*

After installation, run Visual Studio from the Start menu. Then open the Help menu and select About Microsoft Visual Studio. The About Microsoft Visual Studio dialog window should specify at least version 15.7.3, as illustrated in Figure 1-2.

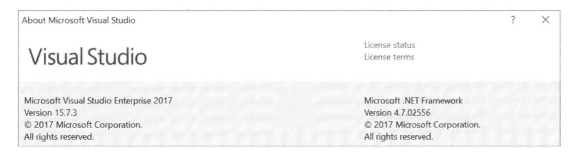

Figure 1-2. *About Microsoft Visual Studio*

ASP.NET Core Blazor Language Services

The Blazor Language Services plugin for Visual Studio will aid you when typing Blazor files and will install the Blazor VS project templates. Installation of the plugin is done directly from Visual Studio. Open Tools ➤ Extensions and Updates. Click the Online tab and enter Blazor in the search box. You should see the ASP.NET Core Blazor Language Services listed as shown in Figure 1-3. Select it and click the Download button to install.

Figure 1-3. *Installing Blazor Language Services from the Extensions and Updates menu*

Visual Studio Code

Visual Studio Code is a free, modern, cross-platform development environment with integrated editor, git source control, and debugger. The environment has a huge range of extensions available, allowing you to use all kinds of languages and tools directly from Code. So, if you don't have access to Visual Studio 2017 (because you're running a non-Windows operating system or you don't want to use it), use Code.

Download the installer from www.visualstudio.com/. Run it and choose the defaults.

After installation I do advise you install a couple of extensions for Code, especially the C# extensions. Start Code, and on the left side, select the Extensions tab, as shown in Figure 1-4.

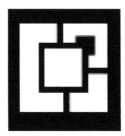

Figure 1-4. *Visual Studio Code Extensions tab*

You can search for extensions, so start with C#, which is the first extension from Figure 1-4. This extension will give you IntelliSense for the C# programming language and .NET assemblies. You will probably get a newer version listed so take the latest.

Click Install.

Another extension you want to search for is Razor+, as shown in Figure 1-5. This extension will give you nice syntax coloring for the kind of Razor files you will use in Blazor.

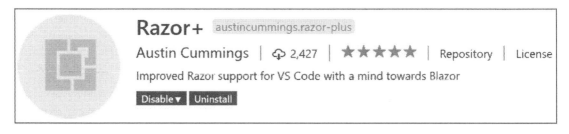

Figure 1-5. *Razor+ for Visual Studio Code*

Installing the Blazor Templates for VS/Code

Throughout this book you will create several different Blazor projects. Not all of them can be created from Visual Studio or Code, meaning you'll need to install the templates for Blazor projects. This section's example shows how to install those templates from the

.NET Core command-line interface, also known as the .NET Core CLI. You should have this command-line interface as part of your .NET Core installation.

Open a command line on your OS, and type the following to install the templates from NuGet:

```
dotnet new -i Microsoft.AspNetCore.Blazor.Templates
```

These templates will allow you to quickly generate projects and items. Verify the installation by typing the following command:

```
dotnet new --help
```

This command will list all the templates that have been installed by the command-line interface. You will see four columns. The first shows the template's description, the second column displays the name, the third lists the languages for which the template is available, and the last shows the tags, a kind of group name for the template. Among those listed are the following:

```
Blazor (hosted in ASP.NET server)        blazorhosted
Blazor Library                           blazorlib
Blazor (Server-side in ASP.NET Core)     blazorserverside
Blazor (standalone)                      blazor
```

Generating Your Project with Visual Studio

With Blazor projects you have a couple of choices. You can create a stand-alone Blazor project (using the `blazor` template) that has no need for server-side code. This kind of project has the advantage that you can simply deploy it to any web server, which will function as a file server, allowing browsers to download your site just like any other site. Or you can create a hosted project (using the `blazorhosted` template) with client, server, and shared code. This kind of project will require you to host it where there is .NET core 2.1 support because you will execute code on the server as well. The third option is to run all Blazor code on the server (using the `blazorserverside` template). In this case, the browser will use a SignalR connection to receive UI updates from the server and to send user interaction back to the server for processing. In this book, you will use the second option, but the concepts you will learn in this book are the same for all three options.

Creating a Project with Visual Studio

For your first project, start Visual Studio and select File ➤ New ➤ Project. On the left side of the New Project dialog, select C# ➤ Web, and then select ASP.NET Core Web Application, as illustrated by Figure 1-6.

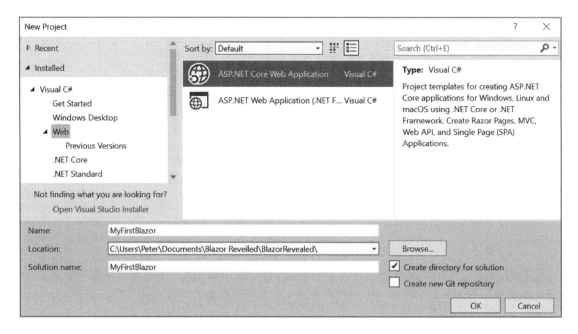

Figure 1-6.   *Visual Studio New Project dialog*

Name your project *MyFirstBlazor*, leave the rest to the preset defaults, and click OK. On the next screen, you can select what kind of ASP.NET Core project you want to generate. From the top drop-downs, select .NET Core and ASP.NET Core 2.1 (or higher), as shown in Figure 1-7. Then select Blazor (ASP.NET hosted) and click OK.

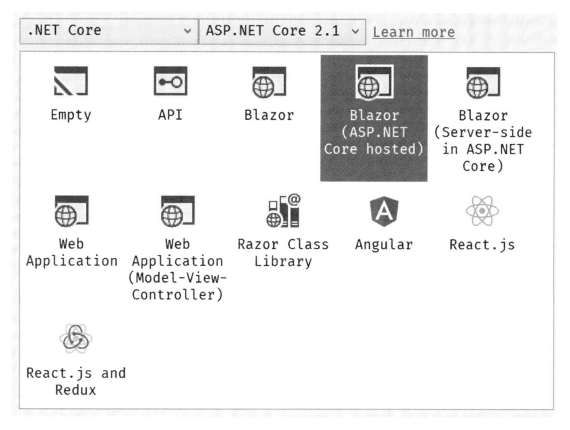

Figure 1-7. *New ASP.NET Core web application*

Wait for Visual Studio to complete. Then build your solution.

At the time of writing this book, Blazor has very limited client-side debugging (and only in Chrome), so running a Blazor project with a debugger just will take more time to show the browser. From now on I will tell you to run without the debugger.

Generating the Project with dotnet cli

To generate the project with dotnet cli, open command line and change the current directory to wherever you want to create the project. Now execute this command to create a new project from the blazorhosted template in the MyFirstBlazor directory:

```
dotnet new blazorhosted -o MyFirstBlazor
```

This command will take a little while because it will download a bunch of NuGet packages from the Internet. When the command is ready, you can build your project using

```
cd MyFirstBlazor
dotnet build
```

Now open your project's folder with Code. When Code has loaded everything, it will pop a little question, as shown in Figure 1-8.

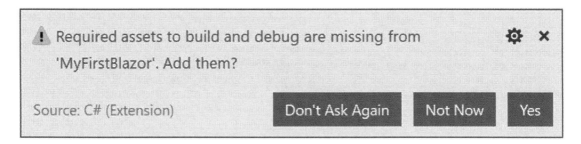

Figure 1-8. *Code asking to add build and debug assets*

Answer Yes. This will add a folder called .vscode with configuration files adding support for building and running the project from Code.

Running the Project

Press Ctrl-F5 to run (this should work for both Visual Studio and Code). Your (default) browser should open and display the home page, as shown in Figure 1-9.

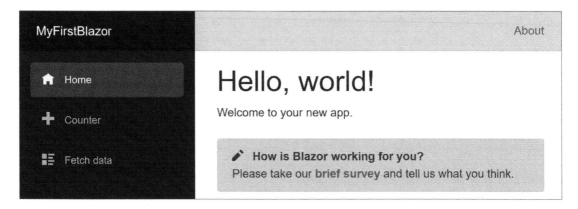

Figure 1-9. *Your first application's home page*

This generated single-page application has on the left side a navigation menu allowing you to jump between different pages. On the right side you will see the selected screen shown in Figure 1-9: the home page. And in the top right corner there is an About link to https://blazor.net/, which is the "official" Blazor documentation web site.

The Home Page

The home page shows the mandatory "Hello, world!" demo, and it also contains a survey component you can click to fill out a survey (please let Microsoft know you like Blazor!).

The Counter Page

In the navigation menu, click the Counter tab. Doing so opens a simple screen with a number and a button, as illustrated by Figure 1-10. Clicking the button will increment the counter. Try it!

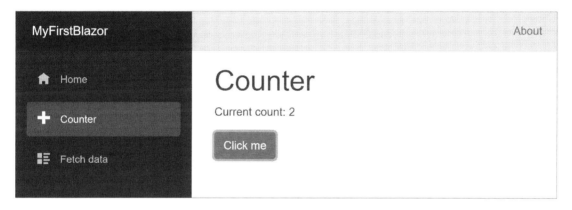

Figure 1-10. *The Counter screen*

The Fetch Data Page

In the navigation menu, click the Fetch data tab. Here you can watch a (random and fake) weather forecast, as shown in Figure 1-11. This forecast is generated on the server when asked by the client. This is very important because the client (which is running in the browser) cannot acccss data from a database directly, so you need a server that can access databases and other data storage.

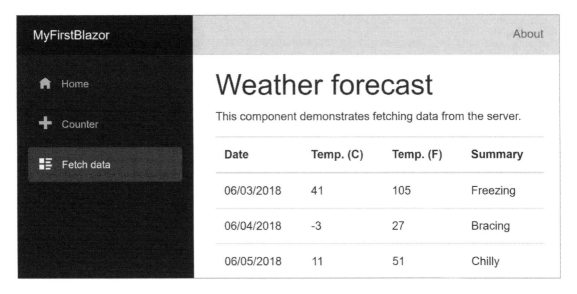

Figure 1-11. *The Fetch data screen*

Examining the Project's Parts

Being able to play with these pages is nice but let's have a look at how all this works. You will start with the server project, which hosts your Blazor web site. Then you will look at the shared project, which contains classes used by both server and client. Finally, you will examine the client project, which is the actual Blazor implementation.

The Solution

Visual Studio and Code use solution files to group projects that will form an application. So a typical Blazor project consists of a server, a client, and a shared project grouped into a single solution. This simplifies building everything since the solution allows tools to figure out in which order to compile everything. Hey, you could even switch between Visual Studio and Code because they both use the same project and solution files!

The Server

Web applications are really a bunch of files that get downloaded by the browser from a server. It is the server's job to provide the files to the browser upon request. There is a whole range of existing servers to choose from, for example IIS on Windows or Apache on Linux. ASP.NET Core has its own built-in server which you generated with the blazorhosted template, which you can then run on Windows, Linux, or OSX.

The topic of this book is Blazor, so I'm not going to discuss all the details of the server project that got generated using the blazorhosted template, but I do want to show you an important thing. In the server project, look for Startup.cs. Open this file and scroll down to the Configure method shown in Listing 1-1.

Listing 1-1. The Server Project's Configure Method

```
// This method gets called by the runtime.
// Use this method to configure the HTTP request pipeline.
public void Configure(IApplicationBuilder app,
                      IHostingEnvironment env)
{
  app.UseResponseCompression();

  if (env.IsDevelopment())
  {
    app.UseDeveloperExceptionPage();
  }

  app.UseMvc(routes =>
  {
    routes.MapRoute(name: "default",
                    template: "{controller}/{action}/{id?}");
  });

  app.UseBlazor<Client.Program>();
}
```

The Configure method is responsible for installing middleware. Middleware are little .NET components that each have a clear responsibility. When you type in a URI, the browser sends a request to the server, which then passes it on to the middleware components. Some of them will take the request and return a response; some of them take the response and do something with it. Look at the first line in the Configure method, shown in Listing 1-2.

Listing 1-2. The UseResponseCompression Middleware

```
app.UseResponseCompression();
```

Your Blazor client will download a lot of files from the server, including .NET assemblies, so compressing these files will result in a faster download. The UseResponseCompression middleware takes care of that.

Would you like to see a detailed error page when the server has an uncaught exception? The UseDeveloperExceptionPage takes care of that. Of course, you don't need it in production (you should handle all exceptions correctly) so this middleware is only used when running in a development environment. How does the server know if you are running in development or release? The if statement you see here checks an environment variable called ASPNETCORE_ENVIRONMENT, and if the environment variable is set to Development it knows you are running in development mode.

The Fetch data screen downloads weather information from the server. These kinds of requests will be handled by the MVC middleware. I will discuss this in more detail in Chapter 5.

The Blazor bootstrap process requires a bunch of special files, especially mono.wasm. They are served by the Blazor middleware, which can be found at the end of the Configure method.

The Shared Project

When you click on the Fetch data tab, your Blazor project fetches some data from the server. The shape of this data needs to be described in detail (computers are picky things); in classic projects, you describe this model's shape twice, once for the client and again for the server because they use different languages. Not with Blazor! In Blazor, both client and server use C#, so you can describe the model once and share it between client and server, as shown in Listing 1-3.

Listing 1-3. The Shared WeatherForecast Class

```
public class WeatherForecast
{
  public DateTime Date { get; set; }
  public int TemperatureC { get; set; }
  public string Summary { get; set; }
```

```
  public int TemperatureF
          => 32 + (int)(TemperatureC / 0.5556);
}
```

The Client Blazor Project

Open the client project's wwwroot folder and look for index.html. The contents of that file should appear as shown in Listing 1-4. To be honest, this looks mostly like a normal HTML page. But on closer inspection you'll see that there is a weird <app> html tag there:

```
<app>Loading...</app>
```

The <app> html element does not exist! It is an example of a Blazor component. You will also see a <script> element:

```
<script src="_framework/blazor.webassembly.js"></script>
```

This script will install Blazor by downloading mono.wasm and your assemblies.

Listing 1-4. index.html

```
<!DOCTYPE html>
<html>
<head>
  <meta charset="utf-8" />
  <meta name="viewport" content="width=device-width">
  <title>MyFirstBlazor</title>
  <base href="/" />
  <link href="css/bootstrap/bootstrap.min.css"
        rel="stylesheet" />
  <link href="css/site.css" rel="stylesheet" />
</head>
<body>
  <app>Loading...</app>

  <script src="_framework/blazor.webassembly.js"></script>
</body>
</html>
```

Routing

What is that <app> element? Open Startup.cs from the MyFirstBlazor.Client project and look for the Configure method, as shown in Listing 1-5. Here you can see the App component being associated with the app tag from index.html. A Blazor component uses a custom tag like <app>, and the Blazor runtime replaces the tag with the component's markup, which is normal HTML recognized by the browser. I will discuss Blazor components in Chapter 3.

Listing 1-5. The Configure Method Associating the app Element to the App Component

```
public void Configure(IBlazorApplicationBuilder app)
{
  app.AddComponent<App>("app");
}
```

The main thing the App component does is install the router, as shown in Listing 1-6. The router is responsible for loading a Blazor component depending on the URI in the browser. For example, if you browse to the / URI, the router will look for a component with a matching @page directive.

Listing 1-6. The App Component

```
<Router AppAssembly=typeof(Program).Assembly />
```

In your current MyFirstBlazor project this will match the Index component, which you can find in the Index.cshtml file, which you can find in the Pages folder. The Index component displays a Hello World message and the survey link, as shown in Listing 1-7.

Listing 1-7. The Index Component

```
@page "/"

<h1>Hello, world!</h1>

Welcome to your new app.

<SurveyPrompt Title="How is Blazor working for you?" />
```

Layout Components

Look at Figure 1-9 and Figure 1-10. Both have the same menu. This menu is shared among all your Blazor components and is known as a layout component. I will discuss layout components in Chapter 7. But how does Blazor know which component is the layout component? Open the Pages folder from the MyFirstBlazor.Client project and look for the _ViewImports.cshtml file. In Razor you use a _ViewImports.cshtml file to define common markup among all razor files in the same folder. If you're familiar with .NET Core, _ViewImports.cshtml from .NET Core is very similar. The Pages folder contains such a file and specifies that all files use the same MainLayout component, as shown in Listing 1-8.

Listing 1-8. Specifying the Layout Component in _ViewImports.cshtml

```
@layout MainLayout
```

In your project, the layout component can be found in MainLayout.cshtml from the Shared folder, which is shown in Listing 1-9.

Listing 1-9. The MainLayout Component

```
@inherits BlazorLayoutComponent

<div class="sidebar">
  <NavMenu />
</div>

<div class="main">
  <div class="top-row px-4">
    <a href="http://blazor.net" target="_blank"
       class="ml-md-auto">About</a>
  </div>

  <div class="content px-4">
    @Body
  </div>
</div>
```

The first `div` with class `sidebar` contains a single component: `NavMenu`. This is where your navigation menu gets defined. You will look in more detail at navigation and routing in Chapter 7.

The next `div` with class `main` has two parts. The first is the About link you see on every page. The second part contains the `@Body`; this is where the selected page will be shown. For example, when you click the `Counter` link in the navigation menu, this is where the `Counter.cshtml` Blazor component will go.

The Blazor Bootstrap Process

Examine Listing 1-4 again. At the bottom you will find the `<script>` element responsible for bootstrapping Blazor in the browser. Let's look at this process.

Go back to your browser and open its developer tools. (Most browsers will open the developer tools when you press F12.) Let's look at what happens at the network layer.

All screenshots in this book use the Chrome browser, mainly because it is available on all platforms (Windows, Linux, and OSX) and because it is very popular with a lot of web developers. If you like another browser better, go right ahead!

Refresh your browser to see what gets downloaded from the server, as shown in Figure 1-12. If Figure 1-12 does not match what you see, clear the browser's cache. Browsers use a cache to avoid reloading files from the server, but when you are developing, you must clear the cache to ensure you are getting the latest changes from the server. First, you will see `index.html` being downloaded, which in turn downloads `bootstrap.css` and `site.css`, and then `blazor.webassembly.js`. A little lower you will see that `mono.js` gets downloaded, which in turn will download `mono.wasm`. This is the mono runtime compiled to run on WebAssembly!

localhost	200	document	Other	567 B	39 ms
bootstrap.min.css	200	stylesheet	(index)	27.2 KB	122 ms
site.css	200	stylesheet	(index)	1.1 KB	122 ms
blazor.webassembly.js	200	script	(index)	11.8 KB	122 ms
open-iconic-bootstrap.min.css	200	stylesheet	(index)	2.5 KB	11 ms
blazor.boot.json	200	fetch	VM116:1	574 B	19 ms
mono.js	200	script	blazor.webassembly....	51.5 KB	35 ms
ng-validate.js	200	script	content-script.js:24	(from disk ...	2 ms
mono.wasm	200	fetch	VM116:1	709 KB	96 ms
favicon.ico	200	text/html	Other	567 B	3 ms
MyFirstBlazor.Client.dll	200	xhr	VM116:1	6.6 KB	8 ms
Microsoft.AspNetCore.Blazor.Browser.dll	200	xhr	VM116:1	19.9 KB	15 ms
Microsoft.AspNetCore.Blazor.dll	200	xhr	VM116:1	45.9 KB	16 ms

24 requests | 1.8 MB transferred | Finish: 1.72 s | DOMContentLoaded: 193 ms | Load: 303 ms

Figure 1-12. *Examining the bootstrap process using the network log*

Now that the .NET runtime is running, you will see that MyFirstBlazor.Client.dll gets downloaded, followed by all its dependencies, including mscorlib.dll and system. dll. These files contain the .NET libraries containing classes such as string, used to execute all kinds of things, and they are the same libraries you use on the server. This is very powerful because you can reuse existing .NET libraries in Blazor that you or others built before!

Summary

Is this chapter, you installed the prerequisites needed for developing and running Blazor applications. You then created your first Blazor project. This project will be used throughout this book to explain all the Blazor concepts you need to know about. Finally, you examined this solution, looking at the server-side project, the shared project, and the client-side Blazor project.

CHAPTER 2

Data Binding

Imagine any application that needs to display data to the user and capture changes made by that user to save the modified data. One way you could build an application like this is to, once you have the data, iterate over each item of data. For example, for every member of a list you would generate the same repeating element, and then inside that element you would generate textboxes, drop-downs, and other UI elements that present data. Later, after the user made some changes, you would iterate over your generated elements, and for every one you would inspect the child elements if their data was changed. If so, you would copy the data back into the objects used for saving that data.

This is an error-prone process, and a lot of work if you want to do this with something like jQuery (jQuery is a very popular JavaScript framework that allows you to manipulate the browser's Document Object Model (DOM)).

Modern frameworks like Angular and React have become popular because they simplify this process greatly through *data binding*. With data binding most of this work for generating the UI and copying data back into objects is done by the framework.

A Quick Look at Razor

Blazor is the combination of *Browser + Razor* (with a lot of artistic freedom). So, to understand Blazor you need to understand browsers and Razor. I will assume you understand what a browser is, since the Internet has been very popular for over more than a decade. But Razor (as a computer language) might not be that clear (yet). Razor is a markup syntax that allows you to embed code in a web page. In ASP.NET Core MVC the code is executed at the server-side to generate HTML that is sent to the browser. But in Blazor this code is executed inside your browser and will dynamically update the web page without having to go back to the server.

Remember the `MyFirstBlazor` solution you generated from the template in the previous chapter? Open it again with Visual Studio or Code and have a look at `SurveyPrompt.cshtml`, as shown in Listing 2-1.

© Peter Himschoot 2019
P. Himschoot, *Blazor Revealed*, https://doi.org/10.1007/978-1-4842-4343-5_2

Listing 2-1. Examining SurveyPrompt.cshtml

```
<div class="alert alert-secondary mt-4" role="alert">
  <span class="oi oi-pencil mr-2" aria-hidden="true"></span>
  <strong>@Title</strong>
  <span class="text-nowrap">
    Please take our
    <a target="_blank" class="font-weight-bold"
       href="https://go.microsofl.com/fwlink/?linkid=873042">
      brief survey
    </a>
  </span>
  and tell us what you think.
</div>
@functions {
[Parameter]
string Title { get; set; } // Demonstrates how a parent
                                component can supply parameters
}
```

As you can see, Razor mainly consists of HTML markup. But if you want to have some C# properties or methods, you can embed them in the @functions section of a Razor file. This works because the Razor file is used to generate a .NET class and everything in @functions is embedded in that class. For example, the SurveyPrompt component allows you to set the Title property, which is set in Index.cshtml, as shown in Listing 2-2.

Listing 2-2. Setting the SurveyPrompt's Title (Excerpt from index.cshtml)

```
<SurveyPrompt Title="How is Blazor working for you?" />
```

Because the Title property can be set in another component, the property becomes a parameter, and because of that you need to apply the [Parameter] attribute, as shown in Listing 2-1. SurveyPrompt can then embed the contents of the Title property in its HTML markup using the @ syntax. This syntax tells Razor to switch to C#, and this will get the property and embed its value in the markup.

One-Way Data Binding

One-way data binding is where data flows from the component to the DOM, or vice versa, but only in one direction. Data binding from the component to the DOM is where some data, like the customer's name, needs to be displayed. Data binding from the DOM to the component is where some DOM event took place, like the user clicking a button, and you want some code to run.

One-Way Data Binding Syntax

Let's look at an example of one-way data binding in Razor. Open the solution you built in Chapter 1 (MyFirstBlazor.sln), and open Counter.cshtml, repeated here in Listing 2-3.

Listing 2-3. Examining One-Way Databinding with Counter.cshtml

```
@page "/counter"

<h1>Counter</h1>

<p>Current count: @currentCount</p>

<button class="btn btn-primary" onclick="@IncrementCount">
  Click me
</button>
@functions {
  int currentCount = 0;
  void IncrementCount()
  {
    currentCount++;
  }
}
```

On this page you get a simple counter, which you can increment by clicking the button, as illustrated by Figure 2-1.

Figure 2-1. *The Counter page*

Let's look at the workings of this page. The `counter` field is defined in the `@functions` section in `Counter.cshtml`. This is not a field that can be set from outside so there is no need for the `[ParameterAttribute]`.

To display the value of the `counter` in Razor, you use the `@currentCount` Razor syntax shown in Listing 2-4.

Listing 2-4. Data Binding from the Component to the DOM

```
<p>Current count: @currentCount</p>
```

Any time Blazor sees that `currentCount` may have been updated it will automatically update the DOM with the latest value of `currentCount`.

Conditional Attributes

Sometimes you can control the browser by adding some attributes to DOM elements. For example, to disable a button you can simply use the `disabled` attribute. Look at Listing 2-5.

Listing 2-5. Disabling a Button Using the `disabled` Attribute

```
<button disabled>On Strike</button>
```

With Blazor you can data-bind an attribute to a Boolean expression (e.g. a property or method of type bool) and Blazor will hide the attribute if the expression evaluates to false (or null) and will show the attribute if it evaluates to true. Go back to the `Counter.cshtml` and add the code from Listing 2-6.

Listing 2-6. Disabling the Click Me Button

```
<button onclick="@IncrementCount"
        disabled="@(currentCount >= 10)">Click me</button>
```

Try it. Clicking the button until the `currentCount` becomes 10 will disable the button. As soon as `currentCount` falls below 10, the button will become enabled again.

Event Handling and Data Binding

You update `currentCount` using the `IncrementCount()` method from Listing 2-3. This method gets called by clicking the Click Me button. This, again, is a one-way data binding, but in the other direction, from the button to your component.

Event Binding Syntax

Look at Listing 2-7. Now you are using the on<event> syntax; in this case, you want to bind to the button's `click` DOM-event, so you use the `onclick` attribute on the `button` element and you pass it the method you want to call.

Listing 2-7. Data Binding from the DOM to the Component

```
<button class="btn btn-primary" onclick="@IncrementCount">
  Click me
</button>
```

Clicking the button will cause the UI to be updated with the new value of the counter. Whenever the user interacts with the site, for example by clicking a button, Blazor assumes that the event will have some side-effect because a method gets called, so it will update the UI with the latest values. Simply calling a method will not cause Blazor to update the UI. I will discuss this later in this chapter.

Event Arguments

In regular .NET, event handlers of type `EventHandler` can find out more information about the event using the `sender` and `EventArgs` arguments. In Blazor, event handlers don't follow the strict event pattern from .NET, but you can declare the event handler method to take an argument of some type derived from `EventArgs`, for example `UIMouseEventArgs`, as shown in Listing 2-8.

23

Listing 2-8. A Blazor Event Handler Taking Arguments

```
void IncrementCount(UIMouseEventArgs e)
```

Using C# Lambda Functions

Data binding to an event does not always require you to write a method. You can also use C# lambda function syntax; see the example shown in Listing 2-9.

Listing 2-9. Event Data Binding with Lambda Syntax

```
<button class="btn btn-primary"
        onclick="@(() => currentCount += increment)">
  Click me
</button>
```

If you want to use a lambda function, you need to wrap it into braces.

Two-Way Data Binding

Sometimes you want to display some data to the user, and you want to allow the user to make changes to this data. This is common in data entry forms. Let's explore the two-way data binding syntax.

Two-Way Data Binding Syntax

With two-way data binding, you have the DOM update whenever the component changes, but the component will also update because of modifications in the DOM. The simplest example is with an `<input>` HTML element.

Let's try something. Modify `Counter.cshtml` by adding an `increment` field and an `input` using the `bind` attribute, as shown in Listing 2-10.

Listing 2-10. Adding an `increment` and an `input`

```
@page "/counter"

<h1>Counter</h1>

<p>Current count: @currentCount</p>
```

```
<button class="btn btn-primary"
        onclick="@IncrementCount">Click me</button>

<input type="number" bind="@increment" />

@functions {
int currentCount = 0;

int increment = 1;

void IncrementCount()
{
  currentCount += increment;
}
}
```

Build and run.

You should now be able to increment the counter with other values, as shown in Figure 2-2.

Figure 2-2. *Adding an increment with two-way data binding*

Look at the input element you just added, repeated here in Listing 2-11.

Listing 2-11. Two-Way Data Binding with the bind Syntax

```
<input type="number" bind="@increment" />
```

Here you are using the bind syntax, which is the equivalent of two different one-way bindings, as shown in Listing 2-12.

Listing 2-12. Data Binding in Both Directions

```
<input type="number"
       value="@increment"
       onchange="@((UIChangeEventArgs e) =>
                    increment = int.Parse($"{e.Value}"))" />
```

This alternative syntax is very verbose and not that handy to use. Using `bind` is much more practical. However, don't forget about this technique; using the more verbose syntax can sometimes be a more elegant solution!

Formatting Dates

Data binding to a `DateTime` value can be formatted with the `format-value` attribute, as shown in Listing 2-13.

Listing 2-13. Formatting a Date

```
<input type="text" bind="@someDate"
                   format-value="dd-MM-yyyy"/>

@functions {

  private DateTime someDate = DateTime.Now;

}
```

In this case, the date will use the European date format. Currently `DateTime` values are the only one supporting the `format-value` attribute.

Reporting Changes

Blazor will update the DOM whenever it thinks changes have been made to your data. One example is when an event executes some of your code, it assumes you've modified some values as a side-effect, and renders the UI. However, Blazor is not always capable of detecting all changes, and in this case, you will have to tell Blazor to apply the changes to the DOM. A typical example is with background threads. Let's look at an example.

Open `Counter.cshtml` and add another button that will automatically increment the counter when pressed, as shown in Listing 2-14. The `AutoIncrement` method uses a .NET `Timer` instance to increment the `currentCount` every second.

Listing 2-14. Adding Another Button

```
@page "/counter"
@using Microsoft.AspNetCore.Blazor.Components

<h1>Counter</h1>

<p>Current count: @currentCount</p>

<button class="btn btn-primary" onclick="@IncrementCount">
  Click me
</button>

<input type="number" bind="@increment" />

<button class="btn btn-success" onclick="@AutoIncrement">
  Auto Increment
</button>

@functions {
  int currentCount = 0;

  int increment = 1;

  void IncrementCount()
  {
    currentCount += increment;
  }

  void AutoIncrement()
  {
    var timer = new System.Threading.Timer((_) =>
    {
      IncrementCount();
    }, null, TimeSpan.FromSeconds(1),
          TimeSpan.FromSeconds(1));
  }
}
```

You might find the lambda function argument in the Timer's constructor a little strange. I use an underscore when I need to name an argument that is not used in the body of the lambda function. Call it anything you want, for example ignore; it does not matter. I simply like to use the underscore because then I don't have to think of a good name for the argument.

Run this page. Clicking the Auto Increment button will start the timer, but the counter will not update on screen. Why? Try clicking the Increment button. The counter has been updated, so it is a UI problem.

Blazor will rerender the page whenever an event occurs. It will also rerender the page in case of asynchronous operations. However, some changes cannot be detected automatically. In this case, you need to tell Blazor to update the page by calling the StateHasChanged method, which every Blazor component inherits from its base class.

Go back to the AutoIncrement method and add a call to StateHasChanged, as in Listing 2-15. StateHasChanged tells Blazor that some state has changed (who would have thought!) and that it needs to rerender the page.

Listing 2-15. Adding StateHasChanged

```
void AutoIncrement()
{
  var timer = new System.Threading.Timer((_) =>
  {
    IncrementCount();
    StateHasChanged();
  }, null, TimeSpan.FromSeconds(1), TimeSpan.FromSeconds(1));
}
```

Run again. Pressing the Auto Increment button will now work.

As you can see, sometimes you need to tell Blazor manually to update the DOM.

The Pizza Place Single Page Application

Let's apply this newfound knowledge and build a nice pizza-ordering web site. Throughout the rest of this book you will enhance this site with all kinds of features.

Creating the PizzaPlace Project

Create a new Blazor hosted project, either using Visual Studio or dotnet cli. Refer to the explanation in the first chapter if you don't recall how. Call the project PizzaPlace. You get a similar project to the MyFirstBlazor project. Now let's apply some changes!

Out of the box, Blazor uses the popular Bootstrap 4 layout framework. However, you can use any other layout framework, because Blazor uses standard HTML and CSS. This book is about Blazor, not fancy layouts, so we're not going to spend a lot of time choosing nice colors and making the site look great. Focus!

In the server project, throw away SampleDataController.cs. You don't need weather forecasts to order pizzas. In the shared project, throw away WeatherForecast.cs. Same thing. In the client project, throw away the Counter.cshtml and FetchData.cshtml files from the Pages folder, and SurveyPrompt.cshtml from the Shared folder.

Your solution should look like Figure 2-3.

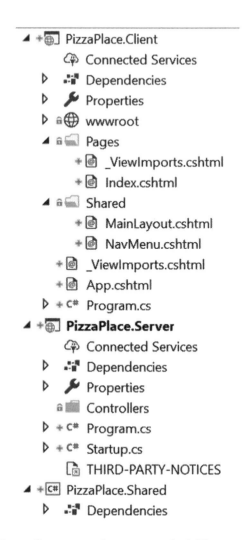

Figure 2-3. *The solution after removing unneeded files*

Adding Shared Classes to Represent the Data

In Blazor, it is best to add classes holding data to the Shared project. These classes are used to send the data from the server to the client and later to send the data back. What do you need? Start with classes representing a pizza and how spicy it is, as shown in Listing 2-16.

Listing 2-16. The Spiciness and Pizza Classses

```csharp
using System;
using System.Linq;

namespace PizzaPlace.Shared
{
  public enum Spiciness
  {
      None,
      Spicy,
      Hot
  }
  public class Pizza
  {
    public Pizza(int id, string name, decimal price,
                 Spiciness spiciness)
    {
      this.Id = id;
      this.Name = name
        ?? throw new ArgumentNullException(nameof(name),
           "A pizza needs a name!");
      this.Price = price;
      this.Spiciness = spiciness;
    }
    public int Id { get; }
    public string Name { get; }
    public decimal Price { get; }
    public Spiciness Spiciness { get; }
  }
}
```

Your application is NOT about editing pizzas, so I've made this class *immutable,* so nothing can be changed once a pizza object has been created. In C# this is easily done by creating properties with only a getter.

Next, you need a class representing the menu you offer. Add a new class to the shared project called Menu with the implementation from Listing 2-17.

Listing 2-17. The Menu Class

```
using System.Collections.Generic;
using System.Linq;
namespace PizzaPlace.Shared
{
  public class Menu
  {
    public List<Pizza> Pizzas { get; set; }
    = new List<Pizza>();
    public Pizza GetPizza(int id)
    => Pizzas.SingleOrDefault(pizza => pizza.Id == id);
  }
}
```

As in real life, a restaurant's menu is a list of meals, in this case a pizza meal.

You also need a Customer class in the shared project with implementation from Listing 2-18.

Listing 2-18. The Customer Class

```
using System;
using System.Collections;
using System.ComponentModel;
namespace PizzaPlace.Shared
{
  public class Customer
  {
    public int Id { get; set; }

    public string Name { get; set; }

    public string Street { get; set; }

    public string City { get; set; }

  }
}
```

Each customer has a shopping basket, so add the `Basket` class to the shared project, as shown in Listing 2-19.

Listing 2-19. The `Basket` Class, Representing the Customer's Order

```
using System.Collections.Generic;

namespace PizzaPlace.Shared
{
  public class Basket
  {
    public Customer Customer { get; set; } = new Customer();

    public List<int> Orders { get; set; } = new List<int>();

    public bool HasPaid { get; set; } = false;

  }
}
```

Please note that you just keep the pizza id in the `Orders` collection. You will learn why later.

One more class before you group them all together. You'll use a `UI` class to keep track of some UI options, so add this class to the shared project, as shown in Listing 2-20.

Listing 2-20. The `UI` Options Class

```
namespace PizzaPlace.Shared
{
  public class UI
  {
    public bool ShowBasket { get; set; } = true;
  }
}
```

Finally, you group all these classes into a single `State` class, again in the shared project with implementation from Listing 2-21.

Listing 2-21. The State Class

```
using System.Linq;

namespace PizzaPlace.Shared
{
  public class State
  {
    public Menu Menu { get; set; } = new Menu();

    public Basket Basket { get; set; } = new Basket();

    public UI UI { get; set; } = new UI();

  }
}
```

There is another good reason to put all these classes into the shared project. There is limited debugging for Blazor, and there is no unit testing framework. By putting these classes into the shared project, you can apply unit testing best practices on the shared classes because it is a regular .NET Core project, and even use the debugger to examine weird behavior.

Building the UI to Show the Menu

With the classes in place to represent the data, the next step is to build the user interface that shows the menu. You will start by displaying the menu to the user, and then you will enhance the UI to allow the user to order one or more pizzas.

Displaying the Menu

The problem of displaying the menu is twofold. First, you need to display a list of data. The menu can be thought of a list, like any another list. Second, in your application, you need to convert the spiciness choices from their numeric values into URLs leading to the icons used to indicate different levels of hotness.

Displaying a List of Data

Open Index.cshtml. Add the @functions section to hold your restaurant's (limited) menu with code from Listing 2-22 by initializing the State instance with a Menu.

Listing 2-22. Building Your Application's Menu

```
@functions {

  private State State { get; } = new State()
  {
    Menu = new Menu
    {
      Pizzas = new List<Pizza>
      {
        new Pizza(1, "Pepperoni", 8.99M, Spiciness.Spicy ),
        new Pizza(2, "Margarita", 7.99M, Spiciness.None ),
        new Pizza(3, "Diabolo", 9.99M, Spiciness.Hot )
      }
    }
  };
}
```

The Pizza Place menu is a list like any other list. You can display it by adding some Razor markup to generate the menu as HTML, as shown in Listing 2-23.

Listing 2-23. Generating the HTML with Razor

```
@page "/"
@using PizzaPlace070.Shared
<!-- Menu -->

<h1>Our selection of pizzas</h1>

@foreach (var pizza in State.Menu.Pizzas)
{
  <div class="row">
    <div class="col">
      @pizza.Name
    </div>
```

35

```
      <div class="col">
        @pizza.Price
      </div>
      <div class="col">
        <img src="@SpicinessImage(pizza.Spiciness)"
             alt="@pizza.Spiciness" />
      </div>
      <div class="col">
        <button class="btn btn-success"
                onclick="@(() => AddToBasket(pizza))">
          Add
        </button>
      </div>
    </div>
}

<!-- End menu -->
```

I like to use comments to show the start and end of each section in my page. This makes it easier to find a certain part of my page when I come back to it later. In the next chapter, you will convert each section in its own Blazor component, making future maintenance a lot easier to do.

What you are doing here is iterating over each pizza in the menu, and generating a row with four columns: one for the name, price, spiciness and finally one for the order button.

Converting Values

You still have a little problem. You need to convert the spiciness value to a URL, which is done by the SpicinessImage method shown in Listing 2-24. Add this method to the @functions area of the Index.cshtml file.

Listing 2-24. Converting a Value with a Converter Function

```
private string SpicinessImage(Spiciness spiciness)
  => $"images/{spiciness.ToString().ToLower()}.png";
```

This converter function simply converts the name of the enumeration's value from Listing 2-14 into the URL of an image file, which can be found in the Blazor project's images folder, as shown in Figure 2-4 (images courtesy from https://openclipart.org). Add this folder (which can be found in this book's download) to the wwwroot folder.

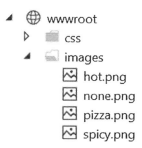

Figure 2-4. *The images folder*

Adding Pizzas to the Shopping Basket

Having the menu functioning leads naturally to the adding of pizzas to the shopping basket. When you click the Add button, the AddToBasket method will be executed with the chosen pizza. You can find the implementation of the AddToBasket method in Listing 2-25. To make debugging easier, you add a Console.WriteLine, which will appear in the browser's console.

Listing 2-25. Ordering a Pizza

```
private void AddToBasket(Pizza pizza)
{
  Console.WriteLine($"Added pizza {pizza.Name}");
  State.Basket.Add(pizza.Id);
}
```

Your Basket class now needs an Add method, shown in Listing 2-26.

Listing 2-26. The Basket's Add Method

```
public void Add(int pizzaId)
{
  Orders.Add(pizzaId);
}
```

Look at the `onclick` event handler for the button from Listing 2-23. Why is this event handler using a lambda? When you order a pizza, you want of course to have your chosen pizza added to the basket. So how can you pass the pizza to `AddToBasket` from Listing 2-25? By using a lambda function, you can simply pass the `pizza` variable used in the `@foreach` loop to it. Using a normal method wouldn't work because there is no easy way to send the selected pizza. This is also known as a *closure* (very similar to JavaScript closures) and can be very practical!

Run the application. You should see Figure 2-5.

Our selection of pizzas

Pepperoni	8.99		Add
Margarita	7.99		Add
Diabolo	9.99		Add

Figure 2-5. The Pizza Place menu

When you click the Add button you're adding a pizza to the shopping basket. But how can you be sure (since you're not displaying the shopping basket yet)?

Open the browser's debugging tools and look at the Console. Each time you click Add, you should see some output from the `Console.WriteLine` in the `AddToBasket` method, as shown in Figure 2-6.

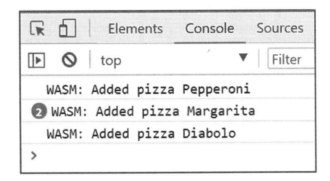

Figure 2-6. Looking at Console.WriteLine's output

Showing the Shopping Basket

The next thing on the menu (some pun intended) is displaying the shopping basket. You are going to use a new feature from C# 7 called tuples. I will explain tuples in a moment. This requires adding the `System.ValueTuple` NuGet package.

Adding a Package with Visual Studio

To add this NuGet package with Visual Studio, right-click the client project and select `Manage NuGet Package`, as illustrated by Figure 2-7. Search for the package and install it.

Figure 2-7. *Installing the System.ValueTuple package with NuGet*

Adding a Package with Visual Studio Code

To add the package with Visual Studio Code, select the `PizzaPlace.Client.csproj` file and add a new package reference:

```
<PackageReference Include="System.ValueTuple"
                  Version="4.5.0" />
```

Displaying the Shopping Basket

Now you are ready to display the shopping basket. Add Listing 2-27 after the menu from Listing 2-21.

Listing 2-27. Displaying the Shopping Basket

```
<!-- End menu -->
<!-- Shopping Basket -->
@if (State.Basket.Orders.Any())
{
  <h1>Your current order</h1>
```

```
@foreach (var (pizza, pos) in
    State.Basket.Orders.Select(
    (id, pos) => (State.Menu.GetPizza(id), pos)))
{
  <div class="row">
    <div class="col">
      @pizza.Name
    </div>
    <div class="col">
      @pizza.Price
    </div>
    <div class="col">
      <button class="btn btn-danger"
              onclick="@(() => RemoveFromBasket(pos))">
        Remove
      </button>
    </div>
  </div>
}
<div class="row">
  <div class="col"> Total:</div>
  <div class="col"> @State.TotalPrice </div>
  <div class="col"> </div>
</div>
}

<!-- End shopping basket -->
```

Most of this stuff is very similar, but now you are iterating over a list of tuples (a very handy new feature in C# 7). Let's look at this code in a little more detail with Listing 2-28.

Listing 2-28. Converting the Shopping Basket for Easy Display

```
@foreach (var (pizza, pos) in
    State.Basket.Orders.Select(
    (id, pos) => (State.Menu.GetPizza(id), pos)))
```

You are using LINQ's Select to iterate over the list of orders (which contain pizza ids). To display the pizza in the shopping basket, you need a pizza, so you convert the id to a pizza with the GetPizza method from the Menu. Please add this method from Listing 2-29 to the Menu class (and a using System.Linq).

Listing 2-29. The GetPizza Method

```
public Pizza GetPizza(int id)
  => Pizzas.SingleOrDefault(pizza => pizza.Id == id);
```

This method converts a pizza id into a pizza using LINQ.

Let's look at the lambda function used in the Select shown in Listing 2-30.

Listing 2-30. Creating Tuples

```
(id, pos) => (State.Menu.GetPizza(id), pos)
```

The LINQ Select method has two overloads, and you're using the overload, taking an element from the collection (id) and the position in the collection (pos). You use them to create tuples. Each tuple represents a pizza from the basket and its position in the basket!

The pizza is used to display its name and price, while the position is used in the Delete button. This button invokes the RemoveFromBasket method from Listing 2-31.

Listing 2-31. Removing Items from the Shopping Basket

```
private void RemoveFromBasket(int pos)
{
  Console.WriteLine($"Removing pizza at pos {pos}");
  State.Basket.RemoveAt(pos);
}
```

And of course, you need to add the RemoveAt method to the Basket class, as shown in Listing 2-32.

Listing 2-32. The Basket Class' RemoveAt Method

```
public void RemoveAt(int index)
{
  Orders.RemoveAt(index);
}
```

At the bottom of the shopping basket the total order amount is shown. This is calculated by the State class. Add the TotalPrice method from Listing 2-33 to the State class. Don't forget to add a using System.Linq statement to the top.

Listing 2-33. Calculating the Total Price in the State Class

```
public decimal TotalPrice
=> Basket.Orders.Sum(id => Menu.GetPizza(id).Price);
```

Run the application and order some pizzas. You should see a current order similar to Figure 2-8.

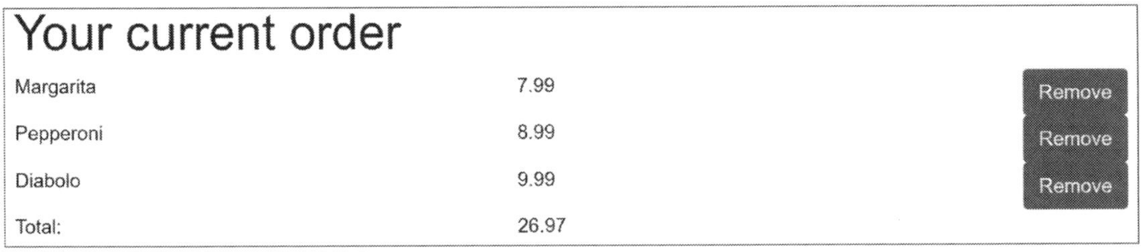

Your current order

Margarita	7.99	Remove
Pepperoni	8.99	Remove
Diabolo	9.99	Remove
Total:	26.97	

Figure 2-8. *Your shopping basket with a couple of pizzas*

Enter the Customer

Of course, to complete the order, you need to know a couple of things about the customer, especially the address because you need to deliver the order.

Start by adding the Razor in Listing 2-34 to your Index.cshtml page.

Listing 2-34. Adding Form Elements for Data Entry

```
<!-- End shopping basket -->
<!-- Customer entry -->
<h1>Please enter your details below</h1>
<fieldset>
  <p>
    <label for="name">Name:</label>
    <input id="name" bind="@State.Basket.Customer.Name" />
  </p>
  <p>
```

```
    <label for="street">Street:</label>
    <input id="street" bind="@State.Basket.Customer.Street" />
  </p>
  <p>
    <label for="city">City:</label>
    <input id="city" bind="@State.Basket.Customer.City" />
  </p>

  <button onclick="@PlaceOrder">Checkout</button>

</fieldset>

<!-- End customer entry -->
```

This adds three labels and their respective inputs for name, street, and city.

You also need to add the PlaceOrder method to your functions, as shown in Listing 2-35.

Listing 2-35. The PlaceOrder Method

```
@functions {

...

private void PlaceOrder()
{
  Console.WriteLine("Placing order");
}

}
```

The PlaceOrder method doesn't do anything yet; you'll send the order to the server later.

Run the application and enter your details, as in Figure 2-9.

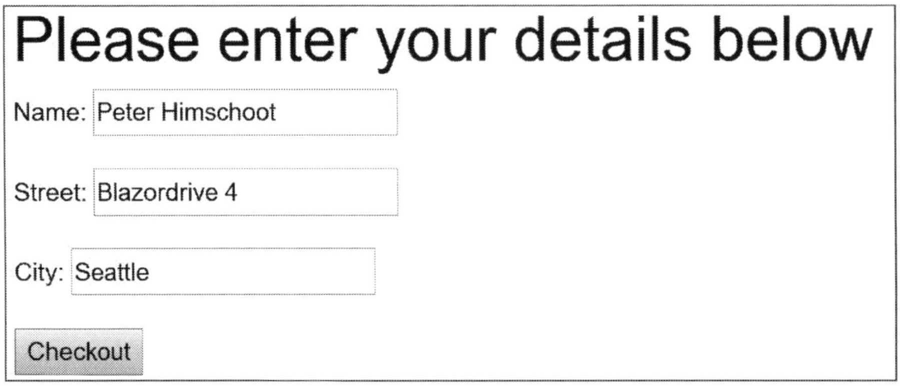

Figure 2-9. *Filling in the customer details*

Debugging Tip

Blazor has limited debugging, and you want to see the State object because it contains the customer's details and order. Will you send the correct information to the server when you press the Checkout button? For this you'll use a simple trick by displaying the state in your page so you can review it any time. Start by adding a new class called DebuggingExtensions to your Blazor project, as shown in Listing 2-36.

Listing 2-36. The DebuggingExtensions Class

```
using Microsoft.AspNetCore.Blazor;

namespace PizzaPlace.Client
{
  public static class DebuggingExtensions
  {
    public static string ToJson(this object obj)
    => Microsoft.JSInterop.Json.Serialize(obj);  }
}
```

And at the bottom of Index.cshtml add a simple paragraph, as shown in Listing 2-37.

Listing 2-37. Showing State

```
<!-- End customer entry -->

<p>@State.ToJson()</p>
```

Run your project. As you interact with the page you'll see State change, with an example shown in Figure 2-10.

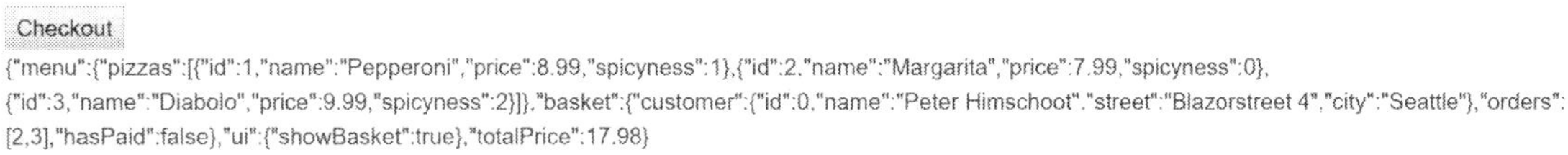

Checkout
{"menu":{"pizzas":[{"id":1,"name":"Pepperoni","price":8.99,"spicyness":1},{"id":2,"name":"Margarita","price":7.99,"spicyness":0},
{"id":3,"name":"Diabolo","price":9.99,"spicyness":2}]},"basket":{"customer":{"id":0,"name":"Peter Himschoot","street":"Blazorstreet 4","city":"Seattle"},"orders":
[2,3],"hasPaid":false},"ui":{"showBasket":true},"totalPrice":17.98}

Figure 2-10. *Watching State change*

It should be obvious that you should remove this debugging feature when the page is ready.☺

Validating the Customer Information

But wait! Clicking the Checkout button works, even while there is no customer name, address, or city! You need to do some validation! So, let's start with an introduction to .NET validation.

Letting Entities Validate Themselves

Classes like Customer should validate themselves because they have the best knowledge about the validity of their properties. .NET has a couple of built-in validation mechanisms, and here you are going to use the standard System.ComponentModel. INotifyDataErrorInfo interface shown in Listing 2-38.

Listing 2-38. The System.ComponentModel.INotifyDataErrorInfo Interface

```
public interface INotifyDataErrorInfo
{
  bool HasErrors { get; }

  event EventHandler<DataErrorsChangedEventArgs> ErrorsChanged;

  IEnumerable GetErrors(string propertyName);
}
```

Its main feature is the GetErrors method, which returns any validation errors for a property as an IEnumerable. As a refresher, IEnumerable and IEnumerable<T> are used by the C# foreach keyword to iterate. The HasErrors property checks to see if there are any errors; it can be used to disable the Checkout button.

Let's make Customer implement the INotifyDataErrorInfo interface. There is one more thing you must do first, however. The HasErrors property of the INotifyDataErrorInfo interface should return a Boolean. An easy way to do this is to simply call the Any extension method from LINQ on the GetErrors method. Unfortunately, this method returns an IEnumerable, and LINQ only works with the newer generic IEnumerable<T> interface. No problem: you can easily build this yourself! Add a new class called IEnumerableExtensions to the shared project with the Any extension method from Listing 2-39.

Listing 2-39. Adding the Any Extension Method to IEnumerable

```
using System.Collections;

namespace PizzaPlace.Shared
{
  public static class IEnumerableExtensions
  {
    public static bool Any(this IEnumerable enumerable)
      => enumerable.GetEnumerator().MoveNext() == true;
  }
}
```

Now implement the INotifyDataErrorInfo interface for the Customer class, as shown in Listing 2-40.

Listing 2-40. The Customer Class with INotifyDataErrorInfo

```
using System;
using System.Collections;
using System.ComponentModel;
namespace PizzaPlace.Shared
{
public class Customer : INotifyDataErrorInfo
{
  ...
```

```csharp
public bool HasErrors => GetErrors(string.Empty).Any();

public event EventHandler<DataErrorsChangedEventArgs> ErrorsChanged;

public IEnumerable GetErrors(string propertyName)
{
  if( string.IsNullOrEmpty(propertyName)
      || propertyName == nameof(Name))
  {
    if( string.IsNullOrEmpty(Name))
    {
      yield return $"A customer's name is mandatory";
    }
    else if( Name.Contains("Pizza"))
    {
      yield return $"Name should not contain \"Pizza\"";
    }
  }
  if( string.IsNullOrEmpty(propertyName)
      || propertyName == nameof(Street))
  {
    if( string.IsNullOrEmpty(Street))
    {
      yield return $"{propertyName} is mandatory";
    }
  }
  if (string.IsNullOrEmpty(propertyName)
      || propertyName == nameof(City))
  {
    if (string.IsNullOrEmpty(City))
    {
      yield return $"{propertyName} is mandatory";
    }
  }
}
}
}
```

I've implemented it to make each property mandatory, and as an extra example, that name should not contain "Pizza" (replace with whatever validation you see fit).

Make sure that the second validation is inside an else clause; otherwise you can get a `NullReferenceException` at runtime!

Note that the `GetErrors` method returns ALL validation errors when you call it with an empty `propertyName`. The `HasErrors` property simply calls `GetErrors` with an empty `propertyName` and then uses your `Any` extension methods to return true if the collection is not empty.

Showing Validation Errors

Now that `Customer` has validation, you can add some UI to show the validation errors as feedback to the user. I don't think I need to explain that this is simply a good (and mandatory) practice! Start by adding validation UI for `Name`, as shown in Listing 2-41.

Listing 2-41. Validation UI for a Customer's `Name`

```
<p>
  <label for="name">Name:</label>
  <input id="name" bind="@State.Basket.Customer.Name" />
  @if (State.Basket.Customer
                  .GetErrors(nameof(Customer.Name))
                  .Any())
  {
    <ul class="validation-error">
      @foreach (string error in State.Basket.Customer
                  .GetErrors(nameof(Customer.Name)))
      {
        <li>@error</li>
      }
    </ul>
  }
</p>
```

Let's discuss this logic. First, you don't need to show any validation UI if there are no validation errors. So, you start by checking if there are any errors for Name. I've repeated this logic in Listing 2-42.

Listing 2-42. Checking If There Are Any Validation Errors for a Customer's Name

```
@if (State.Basket.Customer
            .GetErrors(nameof(Customer.Name))
            .Any())
```

You call GetErrors for the Name property and use the Any extension method to turn it into a Boolean. If there are errors, you use an unordered list to show them, as in Listing 2-43.

Listing 2-43. Using an Unordered List to Show Validation Errors

```
<ul class="validation-error">
  @foreach (string error in State.Basket.Customer
            .GetErrors(nameof(Customer.Name)))
  {
    <li>@error</li>
  }
</ul>
```

The ul element has a validation-error CSS class for styling. Look in the wwwroot folder for the css folder and add (for example) the simple style from Listing 2-44.

Listing 2-44. Adding Some Styling for Displaying Validation Errors

```
.validation crror li {
  color: red;
}
```

Repeat Listing 2-41 for the Street and City properties so you get Listing 2-45.

Listing 2-45. Completing the Validation for Street and City

```
<fieldset>
  <p>
    <label for="name">Name:</label>
    <input id="name" bind="@State.Basket.Customer.Name" />
    @if (State.Basket.Customer
                    .GetErrors(nameof(Customer.Name))
                    .Any())
    {
    <ul class="validation-error">
      @foreach (string error in State.Basket.Customer
                    .GetErrors(nameof(Customer.Name)))
      {
        <li>@error</li>
      }
    </ul>
    }
  </p>
  <p>
    <label for="street">Street:</label>
    <input id="street" bind="@State.Basket.Customer.Street" />
    @if (State.Basket.Customer
                    .GetErrors(nameof(Customer.Street))
                    .Any())
    {
    <ul class="validation-error">
      @foreach (string error in State.Basket.Customer
                    .GetErrors(nameof(Customer.Street)))
      {
        <li>@error</li>
      }
    </ul>
    }
  </p>
```

```
<p>
  <label for="city">City:</label>
  <input id="city" bind="@State.Basket.Customer.City" />
  @if (State.Basket.Customer
                  .GetErrors(nameof(Customer.City))
                  .Any())
  {
  <ul class="validation-error">
    @foreach (string error in State.Basket.Customer
                  .GetErrors(nameof(Customer.City)))
    {
      <li>@error</li>
    }
  </ul>
  }
</p>

  <button onclick="@PlaceOrder" disabled="@State.Basket.Customer.
HasErrors">Checkout</button>

</fieldset>
```

Disabling the Checkout Button

Finally, you don't want to allow the user to click the Checkout button when there are any validation errors. An easy way is to disable the Checkout button. You will use a conditional attribute to set the disable attribute, as shown in Listing 2-46.

Listing 2-46. Using Attribute Binding to Enable/Disable the Checkout Button

```
<button onclick="@PlaceOrder"
        disabled="@State.Basket.Customer.HasErrors">
  Checkout
</button>
```

So as soon as there is a validation error, this button will disable, stopping the customer from placing the order.

Run the site. Your customer should see validation errors in red, as shown in Figure 2-11.

Please enter your details below

Name: [   ]

- A customer's name is mandatory

Street: [   ]

- A customer's street is mandatory

City: [   ]

- A customer's street is mandatory

[Checkout]

Figure 2-11. *Showing validation errors*

Summary

In this chapter, you looked at data binding in Blazor. You started with one-way data binding where you embed the value of a property of field in the UI using the @SomeProperty syntax. You then looked at event binding where you bind an element's event to a method using the on<event>="@SomeMethod" syntax. Blazor also supports two-way data binding where you update the UI with the value of a property and vice versa using the bind="@SomeProperty" syntax. Finally, you examined validation where you can use standard .NET validation techniques like the INotifyDataErrorInfo interface.

CHAPTER 3

Components and Structure for Blazor Applications

In the previous chapter on data binding, you built a single monolithic application with Blazor. After a while, it will become harder and harder to maintain.

In modern web development, we build applications by constructing them from components, which typically are built from smaller components. A Blazor component is a self-contained chunk of user interface. Blazor components are classes built from Razor and C# with one specific purpose (also known as *the principle of single responsibility*) and are easier to understand, debug, and maintain. And of course, you can use the same component in different pages.

What Is a Blazor Component?

To put it in a simple manner, each CSHTML file in Blazor is a component. It's that simple! A Razor file in Blazor contains markup and has code in the @functions section. Each page you in the MyFirstBlazor project is a component! And components can be built by adding other components as children.

Open the MyFirstBlazor project in Visual Studio (or Code) and let's have a look at some of the components in there.

Open index.cshtml (Listing 3-1).

© Peter Himschoot 2019
P. Himschoot, *Blazor Revealed*, https://doi.org/10.1007/978-1-4842-4343-5_3

Listing 3-1. The Index Page

```
@page "/"

<h1>Hello, world!</h1>

Welcome to your new app.

<SurveyPrompt Title="How is Blazor working for you?" />
```

See SurveyPrompt? It is one of the components of the Blazor template. It takes one parameter, Title, which you can set where you want to use the component. Let's have a good look at the SurveyPrompt component.

Examining the SurveyPrompt Component

Open SurveyPrompt.cshtml (see Listing 3-2), which can be found in the Shared folder of the client project.

Listing 3-2. The SurveyPrompt Component

```
<div class="alert alert-secondary mt-4" role="alert">
    <span class="oi oi-pencil mr-2" aria-hidden="true"></span>
    <strong>@Title</strong>

    <span class="text-nowrap">
        Please take our
        <a target="_blank" class="font-weight-bold"
        href="https://go.microsoft.com/fwlink/?linkid=874928">
            brief survey
        </a>
    </span>
    and tell us what you think.
</div>

@functions {
[Parameter]
string Title { get; set; } // Demonstrates how a parent component can
supply parameters
}
```

Look at the Razor markup. This simple component displays an icon in front of the Title, as shown in Figure 3-1, and then displays a link to the survey (which you should take ☺ because it will show Microsoft that you're interested in Blazor).

> ✏ **How is Blazor working for you?** Please take our **brief survey** and tell us what you think.

Figure 3-1. *The SurveyPrompt component*

The @functions code section simply contains property Title, which uses one-way databinding for rendering in the component. Note the [Parameter] attribute. It is required for components that want to expose their properties to the parent component. *Parameters cannot be public properties*, and the compiler will give you an error when you try to make it so.

You might wonder why [Parameter] properties can't be public. I asked Daniel Roth, who's on the Blazor team, and this is his answer: "Think of parameters as like parameters to a method or constructor. They are not something you should generally be able to mutate externally to the component after they have been passed in." Steve Sanderson, who is the key author of Blazor, explains that changing the value of a parameter from code will not behave as expected because change detection will not see the change. Changing the value through data binding shows the change.

Building a Simple Alert Component with Razor

Let's build a simple Blazor component that will show a simple alert. Alerts are used to draw the user's attention to some message, for example a warning.

Creating a New Component with Visual Studio

Open the MyFirstBlazor solution. Right-click the Pages folder and select Add > New Item. The Add New Item window should open, as in Figure 3-2.

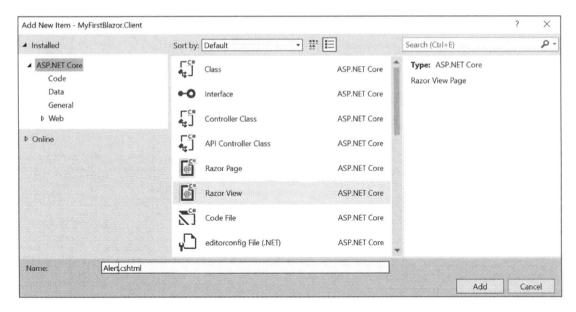

Figure 3-2. *The Add New Item window*

Select Razor View and name it Alert.cshtml. Click the Add button.

Creating a New Component with Code

Right-click the Pages folder of the client project and select New File. Name it Alert.cshtml.

Implement the Alert Component

Remove all existing content from Alert.cshtml and replace with Listing 3-3.

Listing 3-3. The Alert Component

```
@if (Show)
{
  <div class="alert alert-secondary mt-4" role="alert">
    @ChildContent
  </div>
}

@functions {
[Parameter]
bool Show { get; set; }
```

```
[Parameter]
RenderFragment ChildContent { get; set; }
}
```

The Alert component will display whatever content you nest in it (using bootstrap styling).

The default Blazor templates use Bootstrap 4 for styling. Bootstrap (http://getbootstrap.com) is a very popular CSS framework, originally build for Twitter, providing easy layout for web pages. However, Blazor does not require you to use Bootstrap, so you can use whatever styling you prefer. If you so, you must update all the Razor files in the solution to use the other styles, just like in regular web development. In this book, we will use Bootstrap.

The @ChildContent will hold this content and needs to be of type RenderFragment because this is the way the Blazor engine passes it (you will look at this later in this chapter).

Go back to Index.cshtml and add the Alert element. Visual Studio is smart enough to provide you with IntelliSense (see Figure 3-3) for the Alert component and its parameters! Visual Studio Code unfortunately (at the time of writing this chapter) does not offer IntelliSense yet.

Figure 3-3. *Visual Studio IntelliSense support for custom Blazor components*

Complete the Alert and add a button as in Listing 3-4.

Listing 3-4. Using the Alert Component

```
<Alert Show="@ShowAlert">
  <span class="oi oi-check mr-2" aria-hidden="true"></span>
  <strong>Blazor is soo cool!</strong>
</Alert>
```

```
<button class="btn btn-default" onclick="@ToggleAlert">
  Toggle
</button>

@functions {

public bool ShowAlert { get; set; } = true;

public void ToggleAlert()
{
  ShowAlert = !ShowAlert;
}
}
```

Inside the `<Alert>` tag is a `<span>` displaying a checkmark icon and a `<strong>` element displaying a simple message. They will be set as the `@ChildContent` property of the `Alert` component. Build and run your project. When you click the `<button>`, it calls the `ToggleAlert` method, which will hide and show the `Alert`, as shown in Figure 3-4.

Figure 3-4. *The simple* `Alert` *component before clicking the Toggle button*

Separating View and View-Model

You might not like this mixing of markup (view) and code (view-model). If you like, you can use two separate files, one for the view using Razor and another for the view model using C#. The view will display the data from the view model, and event handlers in the view will invoke methods from the view model. Some people prefer this way of working because it's more like the MVVM pattern. Let's try this!

Creating a DismissableAlert Component

If you haven't done this yet, open the MyFirstBlazor solution. With Visual Studio, right-click the Pages folder and select Add ➤ New Item. The Add New Item dialog should open as shown in Figure 3-2. This time select Razor Page and name it DismissableAlert. With Visual Studio Code, right-click the Pages folder, select New File, and name it DismissableAlert.cshtml. Do this again to create a new file called DismissableAlert.cshtml.cs.

A DismissableAlert is an alert with a little x-button that the user can click to dismiss the alert. Replace the markup in the CSHTML file with Listing 3-5.

Listing 3-5. The Markup for DismissableAlert.cshtml

```
@if (Show)
{
<div class="alert alert-warning alert-dismissible fade show"
   role="alert">
  @ChildContent
  <button type="button" class="close" data-dismiss="alert"
          aria-label="Close" onclick="@Dismiss">
    <span aria-hidden="true">&times;</span>
  </button>
</div>
}
```

Replace the C# code in DismissableAlert.cshtml.cs with Listing 3-6.

Listing 3-6. The Code for DismissableAlert.cshtml.cs

```
using System;
using Microsoft.AspNetCore.Blazor.Components;
using Microsoft.AspNetCore.Blazor;

namespace MyFirstBlazor.Client.Pages
{
    public class DismissableAlertViewModel : BlazorComponent
    {
```

```
    [Parameter]
    protected bool Show { get; set; } = true;

    [Parameter]
    protected RenderFragment ChildContent { get; set; }

    public void Dismiss()
    {
        Console.WriteLine("Dismissing alert");
        Show = false;
    }
  }
}
```

Note that the Show and ChildContent properties are now protected properties. Otherwise you will not be able to reference them from the Razor file. Also important is to inherit here from BlazorComponent. We will come back to BlazorComponent later in this chapter.

The DismissableAlertViewModel class will serve as the base class for the Razor file, which you need to indicate with an @inherits at the top of the markup, which you can find in Listing 3-7.

Listing 3-7. Making the CSHTML Inherit from the View Model

```
@inherits DismissableAlertViewModel

@if (Show)
{
<div class="alert alert-warning alert-dismissible fade show"
     role="alert">
  @ChildContent
  <button type="button" class="close" data-dismiss="alert"
          aria-label="Close" onclick="@Dismiss">
    <span aria-hidden="true">&times;</span>
  </button>
</div>
}
```

So instead of putting your code in the @functions section of a Razor file you can put the code in a base class and then inherit from it in the Razor file.

Which model is best? I don't think either one is better than the other; it is more a matter of taste. Choose the one you like.

Referring to a Child Component

Parent and child components typically communicate through data binding. For example, in Listing 3-8 you use DismissableAlert, which communicates with the parent component through the parent's ShowAlert property. Clicking the Toggle button will hide and show the alert. You can try this by replacing the contents of Index.cshtml with Listing 3-8.

Listing 3-8. Using DismissableAlert

```
<DismissableAlert Show="@ShowAlert">
    <span class="oi oi-check mr-2" aria-hidden="true"></span>
    <strong>Blazor is soo cool!</strong>
</DismissableAlert>

<button class="btn btn-default" onclick="@ToggleAlert">Toggle</button>

@functions {

public bool ShowAlert { get; set; } = true;

public void ToggleAlert()
{
    ShowAlert = !ShowAlert;
}
}
```

Instead of using data binding in the interaction between the parent and child component, you can also directly interact with the child component. Let's look at an example. Say you want the alert to disappear automatically after 5 seconds.

Adding a Timer Component

Start by adding a new class called Timer to the Pages folder as shown in Listing 3-9
(the timer will not have any visual part, so you don't even need CSHTML to build the
view). This Timer class will invoke a delegate (Tick) after a certain number of seconds
(TimeInSeconds) have expired. The Tick parameter is of type Action, which is one of the
built-in delegate types of .NET. An Action is simply a method returning a void with no
parameters. There are other generic Action types, such as Action<T>, which is a method
returning a void with one parameter of type T.

Listing 3-9. The Timer Class

```
using System;
using Microsoft.AspNetCore.Blazor.Components;

namespace MyFirstBlazor.Client.Pages
{
  public class Timer : BlazorComponent
  {
    [Parameter]
    protected double TimeInSeconds { get; set; }

    [Parameter]
    protected Action Tick { get; set; }

    protected override void OnInit()
    {
      base.OnInit();

      var timer = new System.Threading.Timer(
        (_) => Tick.Invoke(),
        null,
        TimeSpan.FromSeconds(TimeInSeconds),
        System.Threading.Timeout.InfiniteTimeSpan);
    }
  }
}
```

Now add the `Timer` component to the index page, as shown in Listing 3-10. Let's look at a couple of things. First, you add a reference to the `dismissableAlert` component using the `ref` syntax. This will allow you to reference the component from your code.

Listing 3-10. Adding the `Timer` Component to Dismiss the Alert

```
<DismissableAlert ref="dismissableAlert"
                  Show="@ShowAlert">
    <span class="oi oi-check mr-2" aria-hidden="true"></span>
    <strong>Blazor is soo cool!</strong>
</DismissableAlert>

<Timer TimeInSeconds="5" Tick="@DismissAlert" />
```

Be careful using `<Timer></Timer>`. Any content, even blank spaces, will be seen as `ChildContent`, and since `Timer` doesn't support any you might get compiler errors. It's better to use a single element `<Timer/>`.

This requires that you add a field called `dismissableAlert` of type `DismissableAlert` to the parent, which will contain the reference to the child component, as you can see in Listing 3-11.

Listing 3-11. Using a Field to Refer to the Child Component

```
@functions {
  public DismissableAlert dismissableAlert;

  public bool ShowAlert { get; set; } = true;

  public void ToggleAlert()
  {
    ShowAlert = !ShowAlert;
  }
  public void DismissAlert()
  {
    dismissableAlert.Dismiss();
  }
}
```

Now, when the timer runs out of time, it invokes its `Tick` method, which calls `DismissAlert`. `DismissAlert` calls the `Dismiss` method on the `dismissableAlert` reference, which should then hide the alert.

Run the application and wait at least 5 seconds. The alert does not hide itself! Why?!

Using Component-to-Component Data Binding

So why doesn't your `DismissableComponent` hide itself after 5 seconds?

Look at the markup, which is in Listing 3-10, for `DismissibleAlert` again. It shows the component based on the `Show` parameter, and it gets set through data binding. The problem is that the parent `Index` component's `ShowAlert` stays `true`. Changing the value of the `DismissableAlert` local `show` field will not update the `Index` component's `ShowAlert` property. What you need is two-way data binding between components, and Blazor has that.

With two-way data binding, changing the value of the `Show` parameter will update the value of the `ShowAlert` property of the parent, and vice versa.

Open the `DismissableAlertViewModel` class and change the `Show` property implementation, as shown in Listing 3-12. Here you add an extra parameter that should be called `<<yourproperty>>Changed` and should be of type `Action<<typeofyourproperty>>`.

Listing 3-12. The `DismissableAlertViewModel` Class with Two-Way Binding Support

```
public class DismissableAlertViewModel : BlazorComponent
{
  private bool show = true;

  [Parameter]
  protected bool Show
  {
    get => show;
    set
    {
      if (show != value)
      {
        show = value;
```

```
      ShowChanged?.Invoke(show);
    }
  }
}

[Parameter]
protected Action<bool> ShowChanged { get; set; }

[Parameter]
protected RenderFragment ChildContent { get; set; }

public void Dismiss()
{
  Show = false;
}
}
```

Now whenever someone or something changes the Show property's value, the property's setter triggers the ShowChanged delegate. This means the parent component can inject some code into the ShowChanged delegate property, which will invoke when the property is changed (internally or externally).

Remember to check if the value has changed. This will help you avoid a nasty bug where the child property updates the parent property, which triggers the child property to update, and so on ad infinitum.

Run again. Still, the alert does not disappear. Think about this. You invoke a method asynchronously using a Timer. When the timer fires, you set the ShowAlert property to false. But you still need to update the UI. You could do this by calling StateHasChanged in the DismissAlert method from Listing 3-11. But there is a better way, which is shown in Listing 3-13. Here you call StateHasChanged whenever the ShowAlert property gets a new value.

Listing 3-13. Updating the UI When ShowAlert Changes Value

```
public bool ShowAlert
{
  get => showAlert;
  set
  {
    if (showAlert != value)
    {
      showAlert = value;
      this.StateHasChanged();
    }
  }
}
```

Run. Wait 5 seconds.

The alert should automatically hide, as illustrated by Figure 3-5 and Figure 3-6.

Figure 3-5. *The alert being shown*

Figure 3-6. *The alert automatically hides after 5 seconds*

Building a Component Library

Components should be reusable. But you don't want to reuse a component between projects by copy-pasting the component between them. In this case, it is much better to build a *component library* and, as you will see, this is not hard at all! What you will do here is move the DismissableAlert and Timer component to a library and then you will use this library in your Blazor project.

Creating the Component Library Project

For the moment, you cannot create Blazor component libraries from Visual Studio, so you will have to use the command-line prompt.

Open a command prompt or use the integrated terminal from Visual Studio Code (you can use Ctrl-` as a shortcut to toggle the terminal in Code). Change the current directory to the solution folder. Type in following command:

```
dotnet new blazorlib -o MyFirstBlazor.Components
```

The dotnet new command will create a new project based on a template. The template you want is the blazorlib template. If you want the project to be created in a subdirectory, you can specify it using the -o subdirectory parameter.

Executing this command should show you output like:

```
The template "Blazor Library" was created successfully.
```

Add it to your solution by typing in the next command:

```
dotnet sln add MyFirstBlazor.Components\MyFirstBlazor.Components.csproj
```

This time you want to change the solution, and dotnet sln add allows you to add a project (which is the last argument) to the solution. When you go back to Visual Studio, it will tell you about a file modification, as shown in Figure 3-7.

Simply press Reload to continue working.

Figure 3-7. *Visual Studio detected changes made to the solution*

Adding Components to the Library

Previously, you built a couple of components. Some of them are very reusable, so you will move them to your library project. Start with `Timer`.

Drag-and-drop the `Timer.cs` file from your client project to the components project. You should see a new `Timer.cs` file, as illustrated by Figure 3-8.

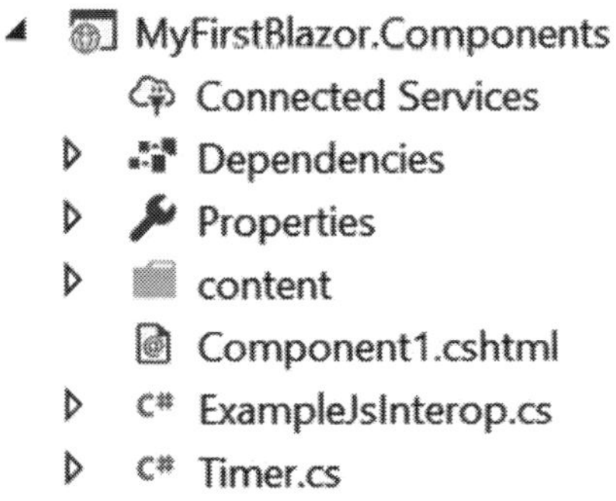

> ◢ 🔲 MyFirstBlazor.Components
>   ☁ Connected Services
>   ▷ ⚙ Dependencies
>   ▷ 🔧 Properties
>   ▷ 🖼 content
>   🗔 Component1.cshtml
>   ▷ C# ExampleJsInterop.cs
>   ▷ C# Timer.cs

Figure 3-8. *Copying the* `Timer.cs` *file to the Components project*

Visual Studio creates a copy of the file, so remove the `Timer.cs` file from the client project (no need to do this with Code). Right-click the `Timer.cs` file in the client project and select `Delete`, as in Figure 3-9.

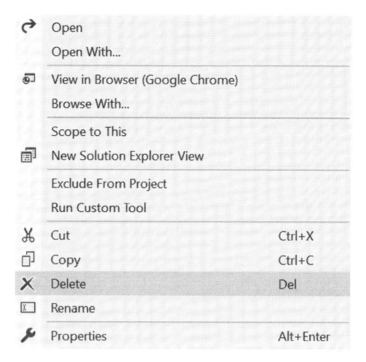

Figure 3-9. *Deleting a file from a project*

Do the same for DismissableAlert.cshtml. Both components are still using the client's namespace, so update their namespace to MyFirstBlazor.Components, as shown in Listing 3-14.

Listing 3-14. Dismissing the Alert

```
@inherits DismissableAlertViewModel

@if (Show)
{
<div class="alert alert-warning alert-dismissible fade show"
     role="alert">
  @ChildContent
  <button type="button" class="close" data-dismiss="alert"
          aria-label="Close"
          onclick="@Dismiss">
    <span aria-hidden="true">&times;</span>
  </button>
</div>
}
```

Building the solution will still trigger compiler errors from the client project because you need to add a reference from the client project to the component library, which you will fix in the next part.

Refering to the Library from Your Project

Now that your library is ready, you are going to use it in your project. The way the library works is that you can use it in other projects. Hey, you could even make it into a NuGet package and let the rest of the world enjoy your work!

Referring to Another Project with Visual Studio

Start by right-clicking your client project and selecting Add ➤ Reference. Visual Studio will show Figure 3-10.

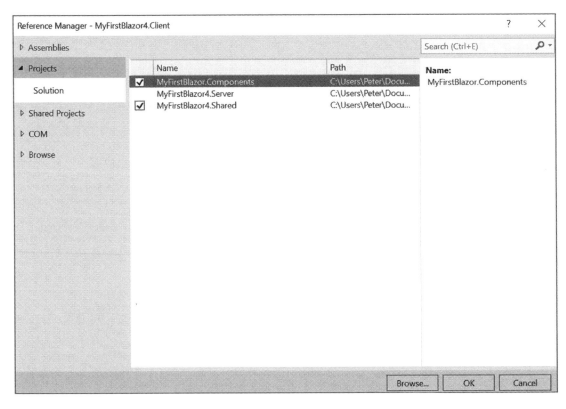

Figure 3-10. *Adding a reference to another project*

Make sure you check MyFirstBlazor.Components and click OK.

Referring to Another Project with Code

Open the MyFirstBlazor.Client.csproj file and add another <ProjectReference>
element to it, as shown in Listing 3-15. It's the last <ProjectReference> from Listing 3-15
you need to add.

Listing 3-15. Adding a Reference to Another Project

```
<Project Sdk="Microsoft.NET.Sdk.Web">

  <PropertyGroup>
    <TargetFramework>netstandard2.0</TargetFramework>
    <OutputType>Exe</OutputType>
    <LangVersion>7.3</LangVersion>
  </PropertyGroup>

  <ItemGroup>
    <PackageReference
      Include="Microsoft.AspNetCore.Blazor.Browser"
      Version="0.5.1" />
    <PackageReference
      Include="Microsoft.AspNetCore.Blazor.Build"
      Version="0.5.1" />
  </ItemGroup>

  <ItemGroup>
    <ProjectReference Include="..\MyFirstBlazor.Shared\MyFirstBlazor.
    Shared.csproj" />
    <ProjectReference Include="..\MyFirstBlazor.Components\MyFirstBlazor.
    Components.csproj" />
  </ItemGroup>

</Project>
```

Now you have added the component library to your project, but if you want to use
the components in your own CSHTML files, you must refer to your component library in
your CSHTML files.

COMPONENTS AND STRUCTURE FOR BLAZOR APPLICATIONS

Understanding Tag Helpers

ASP.NET Core introduced *tag helpers*. Tag helpers are custom elements that get converted to standard HTML elements at runtime. If you use regular ASP.NET Core MVC, the server will convert the tag helpers into HTML, and in Blazor the client will convert tag helpers. As a matter of fact, any Blazor component automatically becomes a tag helper. Visual Studio automatically recognizes tag helpers from the current project, but you need to give it a hand for component libraries, and you do that with @addTagHelper.

Open _ViewImports.cshtml and add the @addTagHelper as in Listing 3-16.

Listing 3-16. Adding Components from a Blazor Library

```
@layout MainLayout

@addTagHelper *, MyFirstBlazor.Components
```

Here you include all custom components using a wildcard (*) from the MyFirstBlazor.Components library. From now on you can use any component from this library as a HTML tag, for example `<Timer/>`.

When you build, you will still get a compile error, and this is because you are using the DismissableAlert type in your functions. And just like any other type, you can either refer to it using its full name including the namespace, or you can add a using statement to Index.cshtml as in Listing 3-17.

Listing 3-17. Adding a using Statement to Refer to Types from the Namespace

```
@page "/"
@using MyFirstBlazor.Components
```

Build and run your solution. It should look like Figure 3-5. Congratulations. You've just built and consumed your first Blazor component library!

Refactoring PizzaPlace into Components

In the previous chapter on data binding you built a web site for ordering pizzas. It used only one component with three different sections. Let's split up this component into smaller, easier-to-understand components and try to maximize reuse.

Creating a Component to Display a List of Pizzas

Open the `PizzaPlace` Blazor project from the previous chapter. Start by reviewing `index.cshtml`. This is your main component, and it has three main sections: a menu, a shopping basket, and customer information.

The menu lists the pizzas and displays each one with a button to order. The shopping basket also displays a list of pizzas (but now from the shopping basket) with a button to remove them from the order. Looks like both have something in common: they need to display pizzas with an action you choose by clicking the button.

Add a new component to the `Pages` folder called `PizzaItem` with contents from Listing 3-18. You can copy most of the markup from the `Index` component with some changes.

Listing 3-18. The `PizzaItem` Component

```
@using PizzaPlace.Shared

<div class="row">
  <div class="col">
    @Pizza.Name
  </div>
  <div class="col">
    @Pizza.Price
  </div>
  <div class="col">
    <img src="@SpicinessImage(Pizza.Spiciness)"
         alt="@Pizza.Spiciness" />
  </div>
  <div class="col">
    <button class="@ButtonClass"
            onclick="@(() => Selected(Pizza))">Add</button>
  </div>
</div>

@functions {
```

```csharp
[Parameter]
protected Pizza Pizza { get; set; }

[Parameter]
protected string ButtonTitle { get; set; }

[Parameter]
protected string ButtonClass { get; set; }

[Parameter]
protected Action<Pizza> Selected { get; set; }

private string SpicinessImage(Spiciness spiciness)
=> $"images/{spiciness.ToString().ToLower()}.png";

}
```

The PizzaItem component will display a pizza, so it should not come as a surprise
that it has a Pizza parameter. This component also displays a button, but how this
button looks and behaves will differ depending on where you use it. And that is why it
has a ButtonTitle and ButtonClass parameter to change the button's look, and it also
has a Selected action that gets invoked when you click the button.

You can now use this component to display the menu. Add a new component to the
Pages folder called PizzaList.cshtml as in Listing 3-19.

Listing 3-19. The PizzaList Component

```razor
@using PizzaPlace.Shared

<h1>@Title</h1>

@foreach (var pizza in Menu.Pizzas)
{
    <PizzaItem Pizza="@pizza" ButtonTitle="Order"
            ButtonClass="btn btn-success"
            Selected="@((p) => Selected(p))" />
}

@functions {
```

```
[Parameter]
protected string Title { get; set; }

[Parameter]
protected Menu Menu { get; set; }

[Parameter]
protected Action<Pizza> Selected { get; set; }
}
```

The PizzaList component displays a Title and all the pizzas from the Menu, so it takes them as parameters. It also takes a Selected action that you invoke by clicking the button next to a pizza. Note that the PizzaList component uses the PizzaItem component to display each pizza, and that the PizzaList Selected action is passed directly to the PizzaItem Selected action. The Index component will set this action, and it will be executed by the PizzaItem component.

With PizzaItem and PizzaList ready, you can use them in Index, which you can find in Listing 3-20.

Listing 3-20. Using the PizzaList Component in Index

```
<!-- Menu -->

<PizzaList Title="Our selected list of pizzas"
          Menu="@State.Menu"
          Selected="@((pizza) => AddToBasket(pizza))"/>

<!-- End menu -->
```

Run the application and try to order a pizza. The shopping basket does not display when you click the Order buttons! Why? Because the UI does not get updated. You need to fix this. You have already seen how to do so. Think about it.

Updating the UI after Changing the State Object

Start by changing the AddToBasket method from Index, as in Listing 3-21. After you add an item to the shopping basket, you call StateHasChanged. This method tells Blazor that it should update the UI with new data.

Listing 3-21. Calling StateHasChanged in AddToBasket

```
private void AddToBasket(Pizza pizza)
{
  Console.WriteLine($"Added pizza {pizza.Name}");
  State.Basket.Add(pizza.Id);
  StateHasChanged();
}
```

Run and order a couple of pizzas. It works!

Think about this. Components rerender themselves after events, but only themselves. When a component makes a change affecting other components, you need to call StateHasChanged on the affected components.

Showing the ShoppingBasket Component

Add a new component called ShoppingBasket to the Pages folder and change its contents to Listing 3-22.

Listing 3-22. The ShoppingBasket Component

```
@using PizzaPlace.Shared

@if (Basket.Orders.Any())
{
  <h1>@Title</h1>

  @foreach (var (pizza, pos) in Pizzas)
  {
    <PizzaItem Pizza="@pizza" ButtonClass="btn btn-danger"
               ButtonTitle="Remove"
               Selected="@(p => Selected(pos))" />
  }

  <div class="row">
    <div class="col"> Total: </div>
    <div class="col"> @TotalPrice </div>
    <div class="col"> </div>
```

```
    <div class="col"> </div>
  </div>
}

@functions {

[Parameter]
protected string Title { get; set; }

[Parameter]
protected Basket Basket { get; set; }

[Parameter]
protected Func<int, Pizza> GetPizzaFromId { get; set; }

[Parameter]
protected Action<int> Selected { get; set; }

protected IEnumerable<(Pizza pizza, int pos)> Pizzas { get; set; }

protected decimal TotalPrice { get; set; }

protected override void OnParametersSet ()
{
  base.OnParametersSet ();
  Pizzas = Basket.Orders.Select((id, pos) => (pizza: GetPizzaFromId(id),
  pos: pos));
  TotalPrice = Pizzas.Select(tuple => tuple.pizza.Price).Sum();
}
}
```

The ShoppingBasket component is similar to the PizzaList component, but
there are some big differences. The basket class keeps track of the order using only
ids of pizzas, so you need something to get the pizza object. This is done through
the GetPizzaFromId delegate. Another change is the OnParametersSet method. The
OnParametersSet method gets called when the component's parameters have been set.
Here you override it to build a list of (pizza, position) tuples that you need during data
binding, and to calculate the total price of the order.

Tuples are just another type in C#. But modern C# offers a very convenient syntax; for example, IEnumerable<(Pizza pizza, int post)> means you have a type that is a list of pizza and position pairs.

Using the ShoppingBasket component in Index is easy, as you can see in Listing 3-23.

Listing 3-23. Using the ShoppingBasket Component

```
<!-- Shopping Basket -->

<ShoppingBasket Title="Your current order"
                Basket="@State.Basket"
                GetPizzaFromId="@State.Menu.GetPizza"
                Selected="@(pos => RemoveFromBasket(pos))" />

<!-- End shopping basket -->
```

Creating a Validation Component Library

The third section of the Index component is about entering and validating details about the customer. You could say that validation is a very common thing, but there is no built-in validation in Blazor so you will create a component library for validation and then use it for building the CustomerEntry component. The Customer class already implements the INotifyDataErrorInfo interface, so this part does not need to change.

Open a command prompt to the folder containing your solution. Type

```
dotnet new blazorlib -o PizzaPlace.Extensions.Validation
```

This creates a new Blazor library project.

Then type

```
dotnet sln add PizzaPlace.Extensions.Validation\
PizzaPlace.Extensions.Validation.csproj
```

This adds the new project to your solution.

Go back to Visual Studio and click Reload. (No need to do this with Code.) Right-click the PizzaPlace.Extentions.Validation project and add a new Razor View called ValidationError and complete is as in Listing 3-24.

Listing 3-24. The ValidationError Component

```
@using Microsoft.AspNetCore.Blazor
@using System.ComponentModel

@if (Errors.Any())
{
  <ul class="validation-error">
    @foreach (string error in Errors)
    {
      <li>@error</li>
    }
  </ul>
}

@functions {

[Parameter]
protected object Subject { get; set; }

[Parameter]
protected string Property { get; set; }

public IEnumerable<string> Errors
{
  get
  {
    switch (Subject)
    {
      case null:
        yield return $"{nameof(Subject)} has not been set!";
        yield break;
      case INotifyDataErrorInfo ine:
        if (Property == null)
        {
          yield return $"{nameof(Property)} has not been set!";
          yield break;
        }
```

```
      foreach (var err in ine.GetErrors(Property))
      {
        yield return (string)err;
      }
      break;
    case IDataErrorInfo ide:
      if (Property == null)
      {
        yield return $"{nameof(Property)} has not been set!";
        yield break;
      }
      string error = ide[Property];
      if (error != null)
      {
        yield return error;
      }
      else
      {
        yield break;
      }
      break;
    }
  }
}
}
```

You expect the Subject and Property parameters to be set to an object implementing either the IDataErrorInfo or INotifyDataErrorInfo interface. You use this to dynamically build the Error collection, which is then used to list any validation errors.

Remember the validation-error style you added in the previous chapter to change the color of validation errors? Move this CSS to the /content/styles.css file from the component library. This concludes the validation component library.

Adding the CustomerEntry Component

Add a reference to the PizzaPlace.Extensions.Validation library, as you saw earlier in this chapter. Now add a new Razor view called CustomerEntry to the Pages folder, as shown in Listing 3-25.

Listing 3-25. The CustomerEntry Component

```
@using PizzaPlace.Shared

@addTagHelper *, PizzaPlace.Extensions.Validation

<h1>@Title</h1>

<fieldset>
  <p>
    <label for="name">Name:</label>
    <input id="name" bind="@Customer.Name" />
    <ValidationError Subject="@Customer"
                     Property="@nameof(Customer.Name)" />
  </p>
  <p>
    <label for="street">Street:</label>
    <input id="street" bind="@Customer.Street" />
    <ValidationError Subject="@Customer"
                     Property="@nameof(Customer.Street)" />
  </p>
  <p>
    <label for="city">City:</label>
    <input id="city" bind="@Customer.City" />
    <ValidationError Subject="@Customer"
                     Property="@nameof(Customer.City)" />
  </p>

  <button onclick="@(()=>Submit(Customer))"
          disabled-"@Customer.HasErrors">Checkout</button>
</fieldset>

@functions {
```

```
[Parameter]
protected string Title { get; set; }

[Parameter]
protected string Title { get; set; }

[Parameter]
protected Customer Customer {get; set; }

[Parameter]
protected Action<Customer> Submit { get; set; }

[Parameter]
protected Action<Customer> Submit { get; set; }
}
```

The CustomerEntry component uses a label and input element for each customer property. You also use a ValidationError component from your freshly built library to display any validation errors. Now you are ready to complete Index with this last component. Listing 3-26 shows the whole Index.cshtml

Listing 3-26. The Index Component

```
@page "/"
<!-- Menu -->
<PizzaList Title="Our selected list of pizzas"
           Menu="@State.Menu"
           Selected="@((pizza) => AddToBasket(pizza))" />
<!-- End menu -->
<!-- Shopping Basket -->
<ShoppingBasket Title="Your current order"
                Basket="@State.Basket"
                GetPizzaFromId="@State.Menu.GetPizza"
                Selected="@(pos => RemoveFromBasket(pos))" />
<!-- End shopping basket -->
<!-- Customer entry -->
<CustomerEntry Title="Please enter your details below"
               bind-Customer="@State.Basket.Customer"
```

```
                Submit="@((_) => PlaceOrder())"/>
<!-- End customer entry -->

@functions {

private State State { get; } = new State()
{
  Menu = new Menu
  {
    Pizzas = new List<Pizza>
{
new Pizza(1, "Pepperoni", 8.99M, Spiciness.Spicy),
new Pizza(2, "Margarita", 7.99M, Spiciness.None),
new Pizza(3, "Diabolo", 9.99M, Spiciness.Hot)
}
  }
};

private void AddToBasket(Pizza pizza)
{
  Console.WriteLine($"Added pizza {pizza.Name}");
  State.Basket.Add(pizza.Id);
  StateHasChanged();
}

private void RemoveFromBasket(int pos)
{
  Console.WriteLine($"Removing pizza at pos {pos}");
  State.Basket.RemoveAt(pos);
  StateHasChanged();
}

private void PlaceOrder()
{
  Console.WriteLine($"Placing order {State.Basket.Customer.ToJson()}");
}
}
```

Build and run the PizzaPlace application. Things should work like before, except for one thing. Remember the debugging tip from the previous chapter? When you change the name of the customer, this tip does not update correctly. Let's fix this. The problem is as follows: when you change the name of the customer, the CustomerEntry component does change the customer's name, but the Index component does not see this change. You can fix this by registering for changes in the customer. To register for changes in objects .NET has the INotifyPropertyChanged interface, which has been part of .NET since .NET 2.0 so you might be familiar with it. This interface is shown in Listing 3-27 and it only has the PropertyChanged event.

Listing 3-27. The INotifyPropertyChanged Interface

```
namespace System.ComponentModel
{
    public interface INotifyPropertyChanged
    {
        event PropertyChangedEventHandler PropertyChanged;
    }
}
```

Whenever a property of customer changes, it should trigger this event. Make the Customer class implement this interface, like in Listing 3-28.

Listing 3-28. The Customer Class Implements INotifyPropertyChanged

```
public class Customer : INotifyDataErrorInfo,
                        INotifyPropertyChanged
```

Now change the Customer's class Name property, as shown in Listing 3-29.

Listing 3-29. The Customer Class' Name Property

```
using System.Runtime.CompilerServices;
...
private string name;
```

```
public string Name
{
    get { return name; }
    set { name = value; OnPropertyChanged(); }
}
```

Whenever the property is modified, you trigger the PropertyChanged event using the OnPropertyChanged method from Listing 3-30.

Listing 3-30. The OnPropertyChanged Method

```
private void OnPropertyChanged(
            [CallerMemberName] string propertyName = "")
{
  PropertyChanged?.Invoke(this,
    new PropertyChangedEventArgs(propertyName));
}
```

I'll explain the implementation a bit. You should pass the name of the property in the PropertyChanged event. You could pass this name as a string to the OnPropertyChanged method, but when you change the name of the property there is a large chance you will forget to update this string. It's better to pass nothing and have the compiler figure out the name of the property. This can be done using the CallerMemberName attribute, which will make the compiler figure out the name of the caller, in this case the name of the property!

Which kind of code is the most maintainable and bug-free code you can write? Code you did not write!

Implement the Street and City properties in the same way.

Almost there. Open Index.cshtml. Add an OnInit method as in Listing 3-31. This method registers for changes in the customer and calls StateHasChanged, which will update the UI. This way you don't need to worry about calling StateHasChanged when a Customer property gets modified.

Listing 3-31. The OnInit Method

```
protected override void OnInit() {
  this.State.Basket.Customer.PropertyChanged +=
    (sender, e) => this.StateHasChanged();
}
```

Build and run. Now when you make a change to the customer the debugging tip will update. You might think, "So what?" The customer could also be used by another component that needs to see changes.

Component Lifecycle Hooks

Every component has a couple of methods you can override to capture the lifecycle of the component. In this section, you will look at these lifecycle hooks because it's very important to understand them very well. Putting code in the wrong lifecycle hook will likely break your component.

OnInit and OnInitAsync

When your component has been completely initialized, the OnInit and OnInitAsync methods are called. Implement one of these methods if you want to do some extra initialization after the component has been created, such as fetching some data from a server, like the FetchData component from the MyFirstBlazor project.

Use OnInit for synchronous code, as shown in Listing 3-32.

Listing 3-32. The OnInit Lifecycle Hook

```
protected override void OnInit()
{

}
```

Use OnOnitAsync (Listing 3-33) to call asynchronous methods, for example making REST calls (you will look at making REST calls in the next two chapters).

Listing 3-33. The OnInitAsync Lifecycle Hook

```
protected override async Task OnInitAsync()
{

}
```

OnParametersSet and OnParametersSetAsync

When you need one or more parameters for initialization, use OnParametersSet or OnParametersSetAsync instead of the OnInit/OnInitAsync methods. These methods get called after the component has been initialized and after the parameters have been data-bound. For example, you could have a DepartmentSelector component that allows the user to select a department from a company, and another EmployeeList component that takes the selected department as a parameter. The EmployeeList component can then fetch the employees for that department in its OnParametersSetAsync method.

Use OnParametersSet (Listing 3-34) if you are only calling synchronous methods.

Listing 3-34. The OnParametersSet Method

```
protected override void OnParametersSet()
{

}
```

Use OnParametersSetAsync (Listing 3-35) if you need to call asynchronous methods.

Listing 3-35. The OnParametersSetAsync Method

```
protected override async Task OnParametersSetAsync()
{

}
```

OnAfterRender and OnAfterRenderAsync

The OnAfterRender and OnAfterRenderAsync methods are called after Blazor has completely rendered the component. This means that the browser's DOM has been updated with changes made to your Blazor component. You can use these methods to invoke JavaScript code that needs access to elements from the DOM (which we will cover in the JavaScript chapter).

Use OnAfterRender (Listing 3-36) to call synchronous methods, for example in JavaScript.

Listing 3-36. The OnAfterRender Lifecycle Hook

```
protected override void OnAfterRender()
{

}
```

Use OnAfterRenderAsync (Listing 3-37) to call asynchronous methods, for example JavaScript methods that return promises.

Listing 3-37. The OnAfterRenderAsync Lifecycle Hook

```
protected override async Task OnAfterRenderAsync()
{

}
```

IDisposable

If you need to run some cleanup code when your component is removed from the UI, implement IDisposable. You can implement this interface in Razor using @implements, as shown in Listing 3-38. Normally you put the @implements at the top of the CSHTML file.

Most of the time, dependency injection will take care of calling Dispose, so generally you won't need to implement IDisposable if you only need to dispose your dependencies.

Listing 3-38. Implementing the IDisposable Interface in a Component

```
@implements IDisposable
```

The IDisposable interface requires you to implement a Dispose method, which you put in @functions, as in Listing 3-39.

Listing 3-39. Implementing the `Dispose` Method

```
@functions {

  public void Dispose()
  {
    // Cleanup resources here
  }
}
```

If you've separated the view and view model, you implement this interface on the view model.

Using Templated Components

Components are Blazor's building blocks for reuse. Blazor also supports *templated components* where you can specify one or more UI templates as parameters, making templated components even more reusable! For example, your application could be using grids all over the place. You can now build a templated component for a `Grid` taking the type used in the grid as a parameter (very much like you can build a generic type in .NET) and specify the UI used for each item separately! Let's look at an example.

Creating the Grid Templated Component

Open the `MyFirstBlazor` project you have been using. Now add a new component (a Razor view) to the `MyFirstBlazor.Client` project's `Pages` folder and name it `Grid` as in Listing 3-40. This is a templated component because it states the `TItem` as a type parameter using the `@typeparam TItem` syntax. This is like a generic type stated in C# with `public class List<T>` where `T` is a type parameter.

You can have more than one type parameter. Simply list each type parameter using the `@typeparam` syntax.

Listing 3-40. The Grid Templated Component

```
@typeparam TItem

<table border="1">
  <thead>
    <tr>@Header</tr>
  </thead>
  <tbody>
    @foreach (var item in Items)
    {
      <tr>@Row(item)</tr>
    }
  </tbody>
  <tfoot>
    <tr>@Footer</tr>
  </tfoot>
</table>

@functions {
[Parameter]
RenderFragment Header { get; set; }

[Parameter]
RenderFragment<TItem> Row { get; set; }

[Parameter]
RenderFragment Footer { get; set; }

[Parameter]
IReadOnlyList<TItem> Items { get; set; }
}
```

The Grid component has four parameters. The Header and Footer parameter are of type RenderFragment, which represents some HTML that you can specify when you use the Grid component (you will look at an example right after exploring the Grid component further). Look for the <thead> element in Listing 3-40 in the Grid component. Here you use the @Header razor syntax to tell the Grid component to put the HTML for the Header parameter here (same thing for the Footer).

The Row parameter is of type RenderFragment<TItem>, which is a generic version of RenderFragment. In this case you can specify HTML with access to the TItem allowing you access to properties and methods of the TItem. The Items parameter is an IReadOnlyList<TItem> which can be data-bound to any class with the IReadOnlyList<TItem> interface. Look for the <tbody> element in Listing 3-40. You iterate over all the items (of type TItem) of the IReadOnlyList<TItem> and you use the @Row(element) Razor syntax to apply the Row parameter, passing the current item as an argument.

Using the Grid Templated Component

Now let's look at an example of using the Grid templated component. Open the FetchData.cshtml component in the MyFirstBlazor.Client project. Replace the <table> (comment the <table> because you will come back to it in later chapters) with the Grid component in Listing 3-41.

The FetchData component uses a couple of things such as @page and @inject. I will discuss them in later chapters, so bear with the example.

The FetchData component uses the Grid component, specifying the Items parameter as the forecasts array of WeatherForecast instances. The compiler is smart enough to infer from this that the Grid's type parameter (TItem) is the WeatherForecast type.

Listing 3-41. The FetchData Component

```
@using MyFirstBlazor.Shared
@page "/fetchdata"
@inject HttpClient IHttp
```

```
<h1>Weather forecast</h1>

<p>This component demonstrates fetching data from the server.</p>

@if (forecasts == null)
{
  <p><em>Loading...</em></p>
}
else
{
  <Grid Items="@forecasts">
    <Header>
      <th>Date</th>
      <th>Temp (Celcius)</th>
      <th>Summary</th>
    </Header>
    <Row Context="forecast">
      <!-- by default called context-->
      <td>@forecast.Date</td>
      <td>@forecast.TemperatureC</td>
      <td>@forecast.Summary</td>
    </Row>
    <Footer>
      <td colspan="3">Spring is in the air!</td>
    </Footer>
  </Grid>

  @*<table class="table">
  ...
  </table>*@
}

@functions {
WeatherForecast[] forecasts;
```

```
protected override async Task OnInitAsync()
{
  forecasts = await Http.GetJsonAsync<WeatherForecast[]>("api/SampleData/
WeatherForecasts");
}
}
```

Now look at the `<Header>` parameter of the `Grid` component in Listing 3-41. This syntax binds whatever is inside the `<Header>` to the `Grid`'s `Header` parameter. In this example, you specify some table headers. The `Grid` puts them inside the `<tr>` element from Listing 3-40. Again, the `<Footer>` is similar.

Examine the `<Row>` parameter in Listing 3-41. Inside the `<Row>` you want to use the current item from the iteration in Listing 3-40. But how should you access the current item? By default, Blazor will pass the item as the `context` argument (of type `TItem`), so you access the date of the forecast instance as `@context.Date`. But you can override the name of the argument, and this is what you do with the `Context` parameters (provided by Blazor) using `<Row Context="forecast">`. Now the item from the iteration can be accessed using the `forecast` argument.

Run your solution and select the Fetch data link from the navigation menu. Admire your new templated component, shown in Figure 3-11!

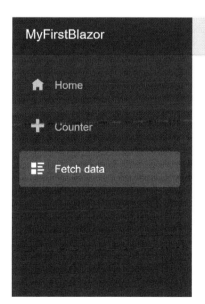

Figure 3-11. *Showing forecasts with the* `Grid` *templated component*

Now you have a reusable `Grid` component that you can use to show any list of items by passing the list to the `Items` parameters and specifying what should be shown in the `Header`, `Row`, and `Footer` parameters! But there's more!

Specifying the Type Parameter's Type Explicitly

Normally the compiler can infer the type of the type parameter, but if this does not work as you expect you can specify the type explicitly. Simply specify the type of your type parameter by specifying it when you use the component, as shown in Listing 3-42.

Listing 3-42. Explicitly Specifying the Type Parameter

```
<Grid Items="@forecasts" TItem="WeatherForecast">
```

Razor Templates

You can also specify a `RenderFragment` or `RenderFragment<TItem>` using Razor syntax. A *Razor template* is a way to define a UI snippet, for example `@<Row>...</Row>`. In this case, you specify a `RenderFragment` without any arguments. But if you need to pass the argument to the Razor template, you use a lambda function. Let's look at an example. Start by adding a new component called `ListView`, as shown in Listing 3-43. This will show an unordered list of items (of type `TItem`) using `<ul>` and `<li>` HTML elements.

Listing 3-43. The `ListView` Templated Component

```
@typeparam TItem

<ul>
  @foreach (var item in Items)
  {
    @ItemTemplate(item)
  }
</ul>

@functions {
[Parameter] RenderFragment<TItem> ItemTemplate { get; set; }
[Parameter] IReadOnlyList<TItem> Items { get; set; }
}
```

Now update the FetchData component as in Listing 3-44. Here you specify the <ListView>'s <ItemTemplate>, which is of type RenderFragment<TItem>, using a Razor template. Look at the forecastTemplate in Listing 3-44. It uses a lambda function, taking the forecast as an argument, which returns a RenderFragment<TItem> using the @<li>...</li> Razor syntax. In the <ListView> component's <ItemTemplate> you simply invoke the lambda function.

Listing 3-44. Using Razor Templates to Specify the Render Fragment

```
@using MyFirstBlazor.Shared
@page "/fetchdata"
@inject HttpClient Http

@{
  RenderFragment<WeatherForecast> forecastTemplate =
    (forecast) => @<li>@forecast.Date.ToLongDateString() - @forecast.
    Summary</li>;
}

<h1>Weather forecast</h1>

<p>This component demonstrates fetching data from the server.</p>

@if (forecasts == null)
{
  <p><em>Loading...</em></p>
}
else
{
  <Grid Items="@forecasts" TItem="WeatherForecast">
  ...
  </Grid>

  <ListView Items="@forecasts" TItem="WeatherForecast">
    <ItemTemplate>
      @forecastTemplate(context)
    </ItemTemplate>
  </ListView>
}
```

```
@functions {
WeatherForecast[] forecasts;

protected override async Task OnInitAsync()
{
  forecasts = await Http.GetJsonAsync<WeatherForecast[]>("api/SampleData/
WeatherForecasts");
}
}
```

Razor templates are a great way to reuse a UI snippet because you can invoke it in different components.

You can also call a Razor template directly in your component as in Listing 3-45.

Listing 3-45. Invoking a Razor Template in Your Component

```
@forecastTemplate(new WeatherForecast {
                  Date = DateTime.Now,
                  TemperatureC = 26,
                  Summary = "Nice!"
              })
```

The Blazor Compilation Model

Every Razor (CSHTML) file gets compiled into C# code and it is very interesting to have a look at them. These files get generated in the `obj` subfolder of your project, and you can look at these generated files from Visual Studio. Select the `PizzaPlace.Client` project in Solution Explorer and click the `Show All Files` button shown in Figure 3-12.

Figure 3-12. *The Show All Files button*

Now open the `obj/Debug/netstandard2.0/Pages` folder in Solution Explorer. Open `PizzaItem.g.cs`, which you can find in Listing 3-46. (I have left out some of the less important details.)

Listing 3-46. The `PizzaItem.g.cs` Generated File

```
namespace PizzaPlace.Client.Pages
{
  public class PizzaItem : BlazorComponent
  {
    protected override void BuildRenderTree(RenderTreeBuilder builder)
    {
      base.BuildRenderTree(builder);
      builder.OpenElement(0, "div");
      builder.AddAttribute(1, "class", "row");
      builder.AddContent(2, "\n  ");
      builder.OpenElement(3, "div");
      builder.AddAttribute(4, "class", "col");
      builder.AddContent(5, "\n    ");
      builder.AddContent(6, Pizza.Name);
      builder.AddContent(7, "\n  ");
      builder.CloseElement();
      builder.AddContent(8, "\n  ");
      builder.OpenElement(9, "div");
      builder.AddAttribute(10, "class", "col");
      builder.AddContent(11, "\n    ");
      builder.AddContent(12, Pizza.Price);
      builder.AddContent(13, "\n  ");
      builder.CloseElement();
      builder.AddContent(14, "\n  ");
      builder.OpenElement(15, "div");
      builder.AddAttribute(16, "class", "col");
      builder.AddContent(17, "\n    ");
      builder.OpenElement(18, "img");
      builder.AddAttribute(19, "src", SpicinessImage(Pizza.Spicyness));
      builder.AddAttribute(20, "alt", Pizza.Spicyness);
      builder.CloseElement();
      builder.AddContent(21, "\n  ");
      builder.CloseElement();
```

```
        builder.AddContent(22, "\n  ");
        builder.OpenElement(23, "div");
        builder.AddAttribute(24, "class", "col");
        builder.AddContent(25, "\n    ");
        builder.OpenElement(26, "button");
        builder.AddAttribute(27, "class", ButtonClass);
        builder.AddAttribute(28, "onclick", Microsoft.AspNetCore.Blazor.
        Components.BindMethods.GetEventHandlerValue<Microsoft.AspNetCore.
        Blazor.UIMouseEventArgs>(() => Selected(Pizza)));
        builder.AddContent(29, ButtonTitle);
        builder.CloseElement();
        builder.AddContent(30, "\n  ");
        builder.CloseElement();
        builder.AddContent(31, "\n");
        builder.CloseElement();
    }

[Parameter]
protected Pizza Pizza { get; set; }

[Parameter]
protected string ButtonTitle { get; set; }

[Parameter]
protected string ButtonClass { get; set; }

[Parameter]
protected Action<Pizza> Selected { get; set; }

private string SpicinessImage(Spiciness spiciness)
=> $"images/{spiciness.ToString().ToLower()}.png";
  }
}
```

As you can see, the bulk of the generated code is the BuildRenderTree method. This method creates elements, attributes, content, and event handlers. For example, the original CSHTML file contains Listing 3-47, which gets generated as Listing 3-48.

Listing 3-47. The Original Razor

```
<div class="col">
  @Pizza.Name
</div>
```

Listing 3-48. The Generated Code from Razor

```
builder.OpenElement(3, "div");
builder.AddAttribute(4, "class", "col");
builder.AddContent(5, "\n     ");
builder.AddContent(6, Pizza.Name);
builder.AddContent(7, "\n   ");
builder.CloseElement();
```

If you really want, you can directly inherit from `BlazorComponent` and override the `BuildRenderTree` method and generate your custom HTML directly here. This is only interesting in some very advanced scenarios which I don't cover in this book.

Summary

In this chapter, you explored building Blazor components and component libraries. You also learned how components can communicate with each other through parameters and data binding. You applied this learning by dividing the monolithic Index component of the PizzaPlace application into smaller components. You also saw that in Blazor you can build templated components, which resemble generic classes. These templated components can be parameterized to render different UIs, which makes them quite reusable! Finally, you had a look at component lifecycle hooks (which you will need in further chapters) and how Razor components get compiled into good old C# code.

Services and Dependency Injection

Dependency inversion is one of the basic principles of *good object-oriented design*. The big enabler is *dependency injection*. In this chapter, you will look into dependency inversion and injection and why they are fundamental parts of Blazer. You will explore them by building a service that encapsulates where the data gets retrieved and stored.

What Is Dependency Inversion?

Currently your Blazor PizzaPlace app retrieves its data from hard-coded sample data. But in a real-life situation this data will be stored in a database on the server. Retrieving and storing this data can be done in the component itself, but this is a bad idea. Why? Because technology changes quite often, and different customers of your application might want to use their own specific technology, requiring you to update your app for every customer.

Instead you will put this logic into a *service object*. A service object's role is to encapsulate specific business rules, especially how data is communicated between the client and server. A service object is also a lot easier to test since you can write unit tests that run on their own, without requiring a user to interact with the application for testing.

But first, let's talk about the dependency inversion principle and how dependency injection allows us to apply this principle.

© Peter Himschoot 2019
P. Himschoot, *Blazor Revealed*, https://doi.org/10.1007/978-1-4842-4343-5_4

Understanding Dependency Inversion

Imagine a component that uses a service. The component creates the service using the new operator, as in Listing 4-1.

Listing 4-1. A Component Using a `ProductsService`

```
@using MyFirstBlazor.Client.Services

<div>
  @foreach(var product in productsService.GetAllProducts())
  {
    <div>@product.Name</div>
    <div>@product.Description</div>
    <div>@product.UnitPrice</div>
  }
</div>

@functions {

  ProductsService productsService = new ProductsService();

}
```

This component is now completely dependent on the `ProductsService`! You cannot replace the `ProductsService` without walking over every line of code in your application where the `ProductsService` is used and replacing it with another class. This is also known as *tight coupling* (see Figure 4-1).

Figure 4-1. *Traditional layered approach with tight coupling*

Now you want to test the `ProductList` component. `ProductsService` requires a server on the network to talk to. In this case, you must set up a server just to run the test. And if the server is not ready yet (the developer in charge of the server hasn't come around to it), you cannot test your component! Or say you are using `ProductsService` in several places in your location, and you need to replace ProductsService with another class. Now you need to find every use of the ProductsService and replace the class. Maintenance nightmare!

Using the Dependency Inversion Principle

The *Dependency Inversion Principle* states

- A.   High-level modules should not depend on low-level modules. Both should depend on abstractions.

- B.   Abstractions should not depend on details. Details should depend on abstractions.

What this means is that the ProductsList component (the higher-level module) should not directly depend on ProductsService (the lower-level module). Instead, it should rely on an abstraction. It should rely on an *interface* describing what a ProductsService should be able to do, not a class describing how it should work.

The IProductsService interface looks like Listing 4-2.

Listing 4-2. The Abstraction as Described in an Interface

```
public interface IProductsService
{
  List<Product> GetAllProducts();
}
```

So change the ProductsList component to rely on this abstraction shown in Listing 4-3.

Listing 4-3. The ProductList Component Using the IProductsService Interface

```
@using MyFirstBlazor.Client.Services

<div>
  @foreach(var product in productsService.GetAllProducts())
  {
      <div>@product.Name</div>
      <div>@product.Description</div>
      <div>@product.UnitPrice</div>
  }
```

```
</div>

@functions {

  IProductsService productsService;

}
```

Now the ProductList component only relies on the IProductsService interface, an abstraction. Of course, you now make the ProductsService implement the interface as in Listing 4-4.

Listing 4-4. The ProductsService Implementing the IProductsService Interface

```
public class ProductsService : IProductsService
{

  public List<Product> GetAllProducts()
  {
      // some implementation
  }

}
```

If you want to test the ProductList component with dependency inversion in place, you can simply build a hard-coded version of ProductsService and run the test without needing a server, as in Listing 4-5. And if you use ProductsService in different places in your application, all you need to do to replace its implementation is to build another class that implements the IProductsService interface and tell dependency injection to use the other class! This is also known as the Open/Closed Principle from SOLID.

Listing 4-5. A Hard-Coded ProductsService Used for Testing

```
public class HardCodedProductsService : IProductsService
{
  public static List<Product> products = new List<Product>
  {
    new Product {
      Id =1,
      Name = "Isabelle's Homemade Marmelade",
```

```
      Description = "...",
      UnitPrice = 1.99M }
  };

  public List<Product> GetAllProducts()
  {
    return products;
  }

}
```

By applying the *Principle of Dependency Inversion* (see Figure 4-2), you gained a lot more flexibility.

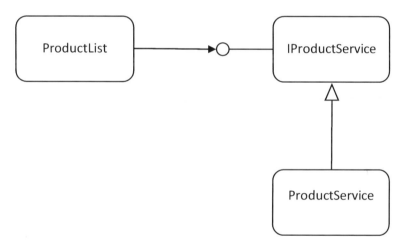

Figure 4-2. *Loosely coupled objects through dependency inversion*

Adding Dependency Injection

If you run your application, now you will get a NullReferenceException. Why? Because the ProductsList component still needs an instance of a class implementing IProductsService! You could pass the ProductsService in the constructor of the ProductList component, for example in Listing 4-6.

Listing 4-6. Passing the `ProductService` in the Constructor

```
new ProductList(new ProductService())
```

But if the `ProductsService` also depends on another class, it quickly becomes like Listing 4-7.

Listing 4-7. Creating a Deep Chain of Dependencies Manually

```
new ProductList( new ProductService(new Dependency()))
```

This is, of course, not a practical way of working! Because of that, you will use *an Inversion-of-Control Container* (I didn't invent this name!).

Applying an Inversion-of-Control Container

An Inversion-of-Control Container (IoCC) is just another object that specializes in creating objects for you. You simply ask it to create an instance of a class and it will take care of creating any dependencies required.

It is a little bit like in a movie when a surgeon, in the middle of an operation, needs a scalpel. The surgeon holds out his or her hand and asks for "scalpel number 5." The nurse (the Inversion-of-Control Container) who is assisting simply hands the surgeon the scalpel. The surgeon doesn't care where the scalpel comes from or how it was built.

So, how can the IoCC know which dependencies your component needs? There are two ways.

Constructor Dependency Injection

Classes that need a dependency can simply state their dependencies in their constructor. The IoCC will examine the constructor and instantiate the dependencies before calling the constructor. And if these dependencies have their own dependencies, then the IoCC will also build them! For example, if the `ProductsService` has a constructor that takes an argument of type `Dependency`, as in Listing 4-8, then the IoCC will create an instance of type `Dependency` and will then call the `ProductsService`'s constructor with that instance. The `ProductsService` constructor then stores a reference to the dependency in some field, as in Listing 4-8. Should the `ProductsService`'s constructor take multiple arguments, then the IoCC will create an instance for each argument. Constructor injection is normally used for *required* dependencies.

Listing 4-8. The `ProductsService`'s Contructor with Arguments

```
public class ProductsService {
  private Dependency dep;

  public ProductsService(Dependency dep) {
    this.dep = dep;
  }
}
```

Property Dependency Injection

If the class that the IoCC needs to build has properties that indicate a dependency, then these properties are filled in by the IoCC. The way a property does this depends on the IoCC (in .NET there are a couple of different IoCC frameworks), but in Blazor you can have the IoCC inject an instance with the @inject directive in your Razor file, as in the third line of code in Listing 4-9.

Listing 4-9. Injecting a Dependency with the @inject Directive

```
@using MyFirstBlazor.Client.Services

@inject IProductsService productsService

<div>
    @foreach(var product in productsService.GetAllProducts())
    {
        <div>@product.Name</div>
        <div>@product.Description</div>
        <div>@product.UnitPrice</div>
    }
</div>

@functions {

}
```

If you're using code separation, you can add a property to your class and apply the [Inject] attribute as in Listing 4-10.

CHAPTER 4 SERVICES AND DEPENDENCY INJECTION

Listing 4-10. Using the `Inject` Attribute for Property Injection

```
using System;
using Microsoft.AspNetCore.Blazor.Components;
using MyFirstBlazor.Client.Services;

namespace MyFirstBlazor.Client.Pages
{
  public class ProductListViewModel : BlazorComponent
  {
    [Inject]
    public IProductsService ProductsService { get; set; }
  }
}
```

You can then use this property directly in your Razor file, as in Listing 4-11.

Listing 4-11. Using the `ProductsService` Property That Was Dependency Injected

```
@inherits ProductListViewModel

<div>
@foreach (var product in ProductsService.GetAllProducts())
{
  <div>@product.Name</div>
  <div>@product.Description</div>
  <div>@product.UnitPrice</div>
}
</div>
```

Configuring Dependency Injection

There is one more thing I need to discuss. When your dependency is a class, the IoCC can easily know that it needs to create an instance of the class with the class' constructor. But if your dependency is an interface, which it generally needs to be if you are applying the Principle of Dependency Inversion, then which class does it use to create the instance? Without your help it cannot know.

An IoCC has a mapping between interfaces and classes, and it is your job to configure this mapping. You configure the mapping in your Blazor project's Startup class, just like in ASP.NET Core. So open Startup.cs, as in Listing 4-12.

Listing 4-12. The Startup Class

```
using Microsoft.AspNetCore.Blazor.Builder;
using Microsoft.Extensions.DependencyInjection;

namespace MyFirstBlazor.Client
{
  public class Startup
  {
    public void ConfigureServices(IServiceCollection services)
    {
      // Configure dependencies here
    }

    public void Configure(IBlazorApplicationBuilder app)
    {
      app.AddComponent<App>("app");
    }
  }
}
```

See the comment? The idea is that you configure the mapping from the interface to the class here, and you use extension methods on the serviceProvider. Which extension method you call from Figure 4-3 depends on the lifetime you want to give the dependency. There are three options for the lifetime of an instance, which I will discuss next.

Figure 4-3. *Configuring dependency injection*

Singleton Dependencies

Singleton classes are classes that only have one instance. They are typically used to manage some global state; for example, you could have a class that keeps track of how many times people have clicked a certain product. Having multiple instances of this class would complicate things because they would have to start communicating with each other to keep tracks of the clicks. Singleton classes can also be classes that don't have any state, that only have behavior (utility classes such as one that does conversions between imperial and metric units). You configure dependency injection to reuse the same instance all the time with the AddSingleton extension method, as in Listing 4-13.

Listing 4-13. Adding a Singleton to Dependency Injection

```
public void ConfigureServices(IServiceCollection services)
{
  services.AddSingleton<IProductsService, ProductsService>();
}
```

Why not use static methods instead of singletons? Static methods and properties are very hard to replace with fake implementations during testing. (Have you ever tried to test a method that uses a date with `DateTime.Now`, and you want to test it with February 29 of some quantum leap year?) However, during testing you can easily replace the real class with a fake class because it implements an interface!

Transient Dependencies

When you configure dependency injection to use a transient class, each time an instance needs to be created by the IoCC it will create a fresh instance. The IoCC will also `Dispose` of the instance (when your class implements the `IDisposable` interface) when it is no longer needed. Most server-side classes should be transient because each request on a server should not depend on previous requests.

However, in Blazor you are working client side, and in that case the UI stays put for the entire interaction. This means that you will have components that only have one created instance and only one instance of the dependency. You might think in this case transient and singleton will do the same thing. But there can be another component that needs the same type of dependency. If you are using a singleton, then both components will share the same instance of the dependency, while with transient each gets their own instance! You should be aware of this.

You configure dependency injection to use transient instances with the `AddTransient` extension method, as in Listing 4-14.

Listing 4-14. Adding a Transient Class to Dependency Injection

```
public void ConfigureServices(IServiceCollection services)
{
  services.AddTransient<IProductsService, ProductsService>();
}
```

Scoped Dependencies

When you configure dependency injection to use a scoped dependency, the IoCC will reuse the same instance per request but will use new instances between different requests. This is especially useful if you use repository objects. Repository objects keep track of all changes made to its objects and then allow you to save (or discard) all changes at the end of the request. If you use transient instancing for repositories, a single request might lose some changes, which would result in subtle bugs. Let's look at an example. Imagine you have a DebitService and another CreditService. Both make changes to a bank account and both use a BankRepository object as a dependency. A TransferService uses a DebitService to debit one account, and the CreditService credits an account, all using the BankRepository. Look at Listing 4-15.

Listing 4-15. Implementing a TransferService

```
public class TransferService {

  private DebitService ds;
  private CreditService cs;
  private BankRepository br;

  public TransferService(
    DebitService ds, CreditService cs, BankRepository br)
  {
    this.ds = ds;
    this.cs = cs;
    this.br = br;
  }

  public Transfer(decimal amount, Account from, Account to) {
    ds.Debit(from, amount);
    cs.Credit(to, amount);
    br.Commit();
  }
}
```

If all three services use the same instance of BankRepository, then this should work fine, as in Figure 4-4.

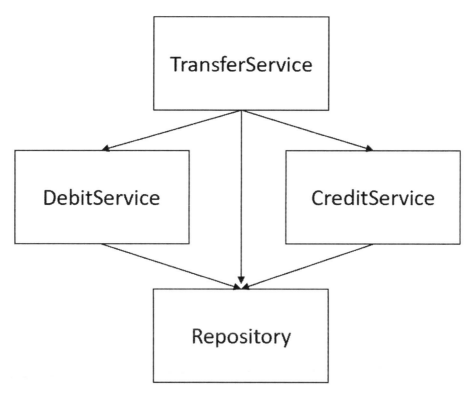

Figure 4-4. *Using a scoped repository*

But if each receives their own new instance of BankRepository, the Commit method will do nothing because no changes were made to the BankRepository instance of the TransferService, as in Figure 4-5.

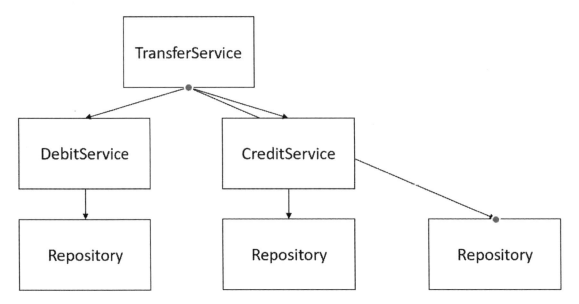

Figure 4-5. *Using a transient repository*

Using scoped dependencies in Blazor will generally be of no practical use, but in the next chapter you will use a scoped instance to implement the microservice.

Never use scoped dependencies inside singletons. The scoped dependency will probably have an incorrect state after the first request.

Disposing Dependencies

One of the nice extras you get with dependency injection is that it takes care of calling the Dispose method of instances that implement IDisposable. If the BankRepository class of the previous example implements IDisposable, cleanup will occur at the end of the lifetime of the instance. In the case of a singleton, this would be at the end of the program; for scoped instances, this would be at the end of the request; and for transient instances, this would normally be when your component is removed from the UI. In general, if your classes implement IDisposable correctly, you don't have to take care of anything else.

Building Blazor Services

Let's go back to your `PizzaPlace` project and introduce it to some services. I can think of at least two services: one to retrieve the menu and one to place the order when the user clicks the Order button.

Start by reviewing the `Index` component, which is shown in Listing 4-16 with the methods left out for conciseness.

Listing 4-16. The Index Component

```
@page "/"

<!-- Menu -->
<PizzaList Title="Our selected list of pizzas"
           Menu="@State.Menu"
           Selected="@((pizza) => AddToBasket(pizza))" />
<!-- End menu -->
<!-- Shopping Basket -->
<ShoppingBasket Title="Your current order"
                Basket="@State.Basket"
                GetPizzaFromId="@State.Menu.GetPizza"
                Selected="@(pos => RemoveFromBasket(pos))" />
<!-- End shopping basket -->
<!-- Customer entry -->
<CustomerEntry Title="Please enter your details below"
               Customer="@State.Basket.Customer"
               Submit="@((_) => PlaceOrder())"/>
<!-- End customer entry -->

<p>@State.ToJson()</p>

@functions {

private State State { get; } = new State()
{
  Menu = new Menu
  {
    Pizzas = new List<Pizza> {
```

```
        new Pizza(1, "Pepperoni", 8.99M, Spiciness.Spicy ),
        new Pizza(2, "Margarita", 7.99M, Spiciness.None ),
        new Pizza(3, "Diabolo", 9.99M, Spiciness.Hot )
    }
  }
};

...
}
```

Pay special attention to the State property. You will initialize the State.Menu property from a service, and you will use dependency injection to pass the service.

Adding the MenuService and IMenuService abstraction

If you are using Visual Studio, right-click the PizzaPlace.Shared project and select Add ➤ New Item. If you are using Code, right-click the PizzaPlace.Shared project and select Add File. Add a new interface class called IMenuService and complete it as shown in Listing 4-17.

Listing 4-17. The IMenuService Interface

```
using System.Threading.Tasks;

namespace PizzaPlace.Shared
{
  public interface IMenuService
  {
    Task<Menu> GetMenu();
  }
}
```

This interface allows you to retrieve a menu. Note that the GetMenu method returns a Task<Menu>; this is because you expect the service to retrieve your menu from a server (you will build this in following chapters) and you want the method to support an asynchronous call.

Let's elaborate on this. Have a look at the OnInitAsync method from Listing 4-20. It is an asynchronous method using the async keyword in its declaration. Inside the OnInitAsync method you call the GetMenu method using the await keyword, which requires GetMenu to return a Task<Menu>. Thanks to the async/await syntax this is easy to do but it does require that you return a task.

Now add the HardCodedMenuService class to the PizzaPlace.Shared project, as in Listing 4-18.

Listing 4-18. The HardCodedMenuService Class

```
using System.Collections.Generic;
using System.Threading.Tasks;

namespace PizzaPlace.Shared
{
  public class HardCodedMenuService : IMenuService
  {
    public Task<Menu> GetMenu()
    {
      return Task.FromResult<Menu>(new Menu {
        Pizzas = new List<Pizza> {
          new Pizza(1, "Pepperoni", 8.99M, Spiciness.Spicy ),
          new Pizza(2, "Margarita", 7.99M, Spiciness.None ),
          new Pizza(3, "Diabolo", 9.99M, Spiciness.Hot )
        }
      });
    }
  }
}
```

Now you are ready to use the IMenuService in your Index component. Start by adding the dependency on IMenuService using the @inject syntax, as in Listing 4-19.

Listing 4-19. Stating That the Index Component Depends on an `IMenuService`

```
@page "/"
@using PizzaPlace.Shared;
@inject IMenuService menuService

<!-- Menu -->
...
```

You initialize the `State.Menu` property in the `OnInitAsync` lifecycle method, as in Listing 4-20. You already have an `OnInit` method from the previous chapter that you don't need any more so don't forget to remove it.

Listing 4-20. Initializing the Index Component's Menu

```
@functions {

  private State State { get; } = new State();

  protected override async Task OnInitAsync()
  {
    State.Menu = await menuService.GetMenu();
    this.State.Basket.Customer.PropertyChanged +=
      (sender, e) => this.StateHasChanged();  }

...
}
```

Never call asynchronous services in your Blazor component's constructor; always use `OnInitAsync` or `OnParametersSetAsync`.

Now you are ready to configure dependency injection, so open `Startup.cs` from the client project. You'll use a transient object, as stated in Listing 4-21.

Listing 4-21. Configuring Dependency Injection for the `MenuService`

```
using Microsoft.AspNetCore.Blazor.Builder;
using Microsoft.Extensions.DependencyInjection;
using PizzaPlace.Shared;
```

```
namespace PizzaPlace.Client
{
  public class Startup
  {
    public void ConfigureServices(IServiceCollection services)
    {
      services.AddTransient<IMenuService,
                            HardCodedMenuService>();
    }

    public void Configure(IBlazorApplicationBuilder app)
    {
      app.AddComponent<App>("app");
    }
  }
}
```

Run your Blazor project. Everything should still work!

Ordering Pizzas with a Service

When the user makes a selection of pizzas and fills in the customer information, you want to send the order to the server so they can warm up the oven and send some nice pizzas to the customer's address. Start by adding an IOrderService interface to the PizzaPlace.Shared project as in Listing 4-22.

Listing 4-22. The IOrderService Abstraction as a C# Interface

```
using System.Threading.Tasks;

namespace PizzaPlace.Shared
{
  public interface IOrderService
  {
    Task PlaceOrder(Basket basket);
  }
}
```

To place an order, you just send the basket to the server. In the next chapter, you will build the actual server-side code to place an order; for now, you will use a fake implementation that simply writes the order to the browser's console. Add a class called ConsoleOrderService to the PizzaPlace.Shared project as in Listing 4-23.

Listing 4-23. The ConsoleOrderService

```
using System;
using System.Threading.Tasks;

namespace PizzaPlace.Shared
{
  public class ConsoleOrderService : IOrderService
  {
    public Task PlaceOrder(Basket basket)
    {
      Console.WriteLine($"Placing order for {basket.Customer.Name}");
      return Task.CompletedTask;
    }
  }
}
```

The PlaceOrder method simply writes the basket to the console. However, this method implements the asynchronous pattern from .NET, so you need to return a Task instance. This is easily done using the Task.CompletedTask property. Task.CompletedTask is simply a "no nothing" task and is very handy if you need to implement a method that needs to return a Task instance.

Inject the IOrderService into the Index component as in Listing 4-24.

Listing 4-24. Injecting the IOrderService

```
@page "/"
@using PizzaPlace.Shared;
@inject IMenuService  menuService
@inject IOrderService  orderService
```

Use the order service when the user clicks on the Order button by replacing the implementation of the `PlaceOrder` method in the Index component. Since the `orderService` is asynchronous, you need to invoke it in an asynchronous way, as in Listing 4-25.

Listing 4-25. The Asynchronous `PlaceOrder` Method

```
private async Task PlaceOrder()
{
  await orderService.PlaceOrder(State.Basket);
}
```

As the final step, configure dependency injection. Again, make the `orderService` transient as in Listing 4-26.

Listing 4-26. Configuring Dependency Injection for the `orderService`

```
using Microsoft.AspNetCore.Blazor.Builder;
using Microsoft.Extensions.DependencyInjection;
using PizzaPlace.Shared;

namespace PizzaPlace.Client
{
  public class Startup
  {
    public void ConfigureServices(IServiceCollection services)
    {
      services.AddTransient<IMenuService,
                            HardCodedMenuService>();
      services.AddTransient<IOrderService,
                            ConsoleOrderService>();
    }

    public void Configure(IBlazorApplicationBuilder app)
    {
      app.AddComponent<App>("app");
    }
  }
}
```

Think about this. How hard will it be to replace the implementation of one of the services? There is only one place that says which class you will be using, and that is in Listing 4-26. In the next chapter, you will build the server-side code needed to store the menu and the orders, and in the chapter after that you will replace these services with the real deal!

Build your project. You will get a warning about making a call to an asynchronous method. This is because the IOrderService's PlaceOrder method is now asynchronous. Fix it by changing the CustomerEntry's Submit property to use an asynchronous lambda function as in Listing 4-27.

Listing 4-27. Changing to an Asynchronous Lambda Function

```
<!-- Customer entry -->
<CustomerEntry Title="Please enter your details below"
               Customer="@State.Basket.Customer"
               Submit="@(async (_) => await PlaceOrder())"/>
<!-- End customer entry -->
```

Build and run your project again, open your browser's debugger, and open the console tab. Order some pizzas and click the Order button. You should see some feedback, as shown in Figure 4-6.

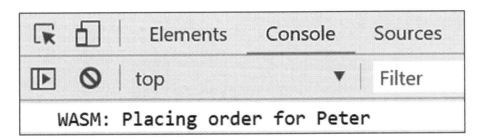

Figure 4-6. *The brower's console showing that an order was placed*

Summary

In this chapter you learned about dependency inversion, which is a best practice for building easily maintainable and testable object-oriented applications. You also saw that dependency injection makes it very easy to create objects with dependencies, especially objects that use dependency inversion. When you configure dependency injection, you need to be careful with the lifetime of your instances, so let's repeat that again:

- *Transient* objects are always different; a new instance is provided to every component and every service.

- *Scoped* objects are the same within a request but different across different requests.

- *Singleton* objects are the same for every object and every request.

CHAPTER 5

Data Storage and Microservices

In general, client-side browser applications need to store some of their data. In some cases, such as games, the application can store its data in the browser itself, using browser local storage. But in most cases storage will happen on the server, which has access to database engines such as SQL Server. In this chapter, you will learn the basics of storing data using Entity Framework Core and exposing that data using REST and microservices built on top of ASP.NET Core.

What Is REST?

Storing data on the Web is ubiquitous. But how can applications communicate with one another? *Representational State Transfer* (REST) is a protocol built on top of the HTTP protocol for invoking functionality on servers, such as retrieving and storing data from/ in a database.

Understanding HTTP

Before talking about REST, you should have a good understanding of the *Hypertext Transfer Protocol*, better known as HTTP. HTTP was created by *Tim Berners-Lee* at CERN in 1989. CERN is a center for elementary physics research, and what do researchers do when they have completed their research? They publish papers with their research's findings. Before the Internet, publishing a paper was done literally on paper (hence the name) and it took a lot of time between writing the paper and getting it published in a research magazine. Instead, Tim Berners-Lee devised a way to put papers on a server and allow users to read these papers using a browser.

© Peter Himschoot 2019
P. Himschoot, *Blazor Revealed*, https://doi.org/10.1007/978-1-4842-4343-5_5

Also, scientific papers contain a lot of references, and when you want to read a paper like this it helps to be able to access the referenced papers. The Internet facilitates reading papers through the use to *Hypertext Markup Language* (HTML). Hypertext is an electronic document format that can contain links to other documents. You simply click the link to read the other paper and you can go back to the first paper simply by clicking the back button in your browser.

Universal Resource Identifiers and Verbs

Browsers are applications that know how to talk HTTP, and the first thing you do after opening a browser is you type in a *Universal Resource Identifier* (URI). A URI allows a browser to talk to a server, but more is needed. As the name suggests, a URI identifies some resource universally, but you also need to use a *verb* to instruct the server to do something with the URI. The most common verb is GET. As Figure 5-1 shows, when you type in a URI in the browser, it will do a GET on the server.

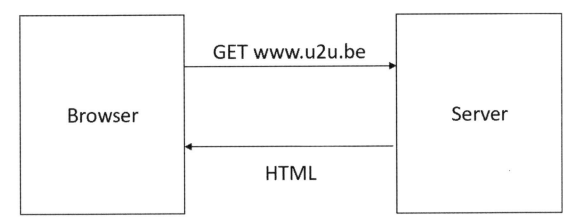

Figure 5-1. *The browser uses the GET verb to retrieve a document*

Each time you click a hyperlink in the HTML document, the browser repeats this process with another URI.

But there are other verbs. If you want to publish a new paper, you can use the POST verb to send the paper to the server, supplying it with a URI. In this case, the server will store the paper at the requested URI. If you want to make a change to your paper, for example to correct a spelling mistake, you can use the PUT verb. Now the server will overwrite the URI contents. And finally, you can delete the paper using the DELETE verb and its URI.

HTTP Status Codes

What happens when you ask a server about something it doesn't have? What should the server return? Servers not only return HTML, they also return a status code about the result. When the server can process the request successfully, it will in general return status code 200 (other successful status codes exist). When the server can't find the resource, it will return a status code 404. Status code 404 simply means not found. The client will receive this status code and can react appropriately. When the browser receives a status code 200, it displays the HTML; when it receives a 404, it displays a not found screen, etc.

Invoking Server Functionality Using REST

Think about these verbs we just talked about. With POST you can CREATE something on a server; with GET you can READ it back; with PUT you can UPDATE something on the server; and with DELETE you can DELETE something on the server. They are also known as CRUD operations (CREATE-READ-UPDATE-DELETE). *Roy Fielding*, the inventor of REST, realized that using the HTTP protocol you can also use HTTP to work with data stored in a database. For example, if you use the GET verb with a URI `http://someserver/categories`, the server can execute some code to retrieve data from the categories relational table and return it. Of course, the server would use a format more appropriate for transferring data, such as XML or JSON. Because there are many different formats for data, the server also needs a way to convey which format it is sending. (In the beginning of the Web only HTML was used as the format.) This is done through HTTP headers.

HTTP Headers

HTTP headers are instructions exchanged between the client and the server. Headers are key-value pairs, where client and server agree on the key. Many standard HTTP headers exist. For example, a server can use the *Content-Type header* to tell the client to expect a specific format. Another header is the *Accept header*, which is sent by the client to the server to politely ask the server to send the content in that format; this is also known as *content negotiation*. Currently the most popular format is *JavaScript Object Notation* (JSON). And this is the exchange format you will use with Blazor.

JavaScript Object Notation

JSON is a compact format for transferring data. Look at the example in Listing 5-1.

Listing 5-1. An Example of JSON

```
{ "book" : {
  "title" : "Blazor Revealed",
  "chapters" : [ "Your first Blazor project", "Data Binding"]
  }
}
```

This JSON format describes a book, an object in memory. Objects are denoted using curly braces. Inside the book are two properties; each property uses a `key : value` notation. The book's `title` is `"Blazor Revealed."` Note that the property name is also transferred as a string. And finally, the `chapters` property is an array of strings, where you use square brackets to indicate an array.

The JSON format is used for transferring data between two machines, but today is also heavily used for configuring tools such as ASP.NET Core. JSON today is way more popular on the Web than XML, probably because of its simplicity.

Some Examples of REST Calls

You need a list of pizzas from a server, and the server exposes the pizzas at URI `http://someserver/pizzas`. To get a list of pizzas, you use the GET verb, and you use the `Accept` header with value `application/json` to request the JSON format. Look at Figure 5-2 for this example.

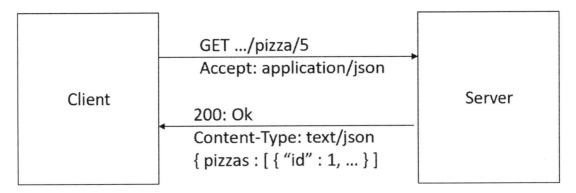

Figure 5-2. *Using REST to retrieve a list of pizzas*

Maybe your client wants to display the details of a pizza with id number 5. In this case, it can append the id to the URI and perform a GET. Should the server not have any pizza with that id, it can return a status code 404, as illustrated in Figure 5-3.

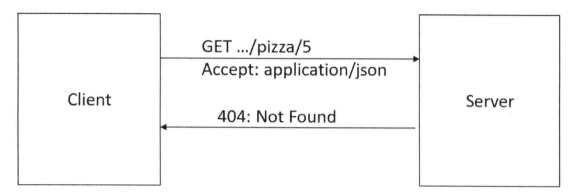

Figure 5-3. *Using REST to retrieve a specific pizza through its unique id*

As a last example, let's send some data from the client to the server. Imagine that the customer has filled in all the details for the order and clicks the Order button. You then send the order as JSON to the server using the POST verb (remember POST means insert). The server can then process the order in any way it likes; for instance, it can insert the order into its database and return a 201: Created status code, as in Figure 5-4. REST recommends returning a 201 status code with the Location header set to the URI for the newly created resource.

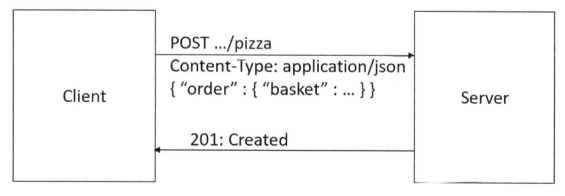

Figure 5-4. *POSTing an order to the server*

Building a Simple Microservice Using ASP.NET Core

So, how do you build a REST service? Your Blazor project uses ASP.NET Core for hosting the Blazor client and adding a service to your project is easy. But first, let's do a little intro to microservices.

Services and Single Responsibility

A service is a piece of software that listens for requests; when it receives a request, the service handles the request and returns with a response. In real life, you also encounter services and they are very similar. Consider a bank. You step into a bank and you give the teller your account number, some ID, and request $100. The teller will check your account; if you have enough money in your account, the teller will deduct the money and give you the cash. Should your account be too low, the teller will refuse. In both cases, you got a response.

Services should also adhere to the principle of single responsibility. They should do one thing very well, and that's it. For example, the pizza service will allow clients to retrieve pizzas, add, update, and delete pizzas. That's it. A single responsibility, in this case PIZZAS.

You can have other services too, each with their own responsibility. Services that take care of one thing are known as *microservices*.

The Pizza Service

Open the PizzaPlace solution you worked on in previous chapters. In this chapter, you will focus on the `PizzaPlace.Server` project, shown in Figure 5-5.

Figure 5-5. *The PizzaPlace.Server project*

The only role this project currently has is to host your Blazor client application, but now you will enhance this role by adding some microservices.

Open Startup.cs and look at the Configure method, as in Listing 5-2.

Listing 5-2. The Startup Class' Configure Method

```
public void Configure(IApplicationBuilder app,
                      IHostingEnvironment env)
{
  app.UseResponseCompression();

  if (env.IsDevelopment())
  {
    app.UseDeveloperExceptionPage();
  }

  app.UseMvc(routes =>
  {
```

```
    routes.MapRoute(name: "default",
                    template: "{controller}/{action}/{id?}");
  });

  app.UseBlazor<Client.Program>();
}
```

The last line with the UseBlazor method takes care of your Blazor Client project. But right before it you see the UseMvc method that it used for hosting your services.

How the UseMvc method works is not the topic of this book, but I will cover what you need to know. If you want to learn more about ASP.NET Core, there are many good books about this topic, such as *Pro ASP.NET Core MVC* by Adam Freeman.

Next in line is the Controllers folder. In Figure 5-5 this folder is empty, and the idea is that you put your service classes here. In ASP.NET, service classes are known as controllers. If you are using Visual Studio, right-click this folder and select Add ➤ Controller. Select API Controller - Empty from Figure 5-6 and click Add.

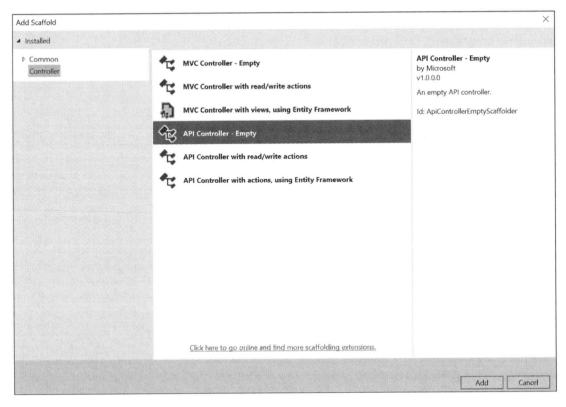

Figure 5-6. *Adding a new controller*

Type PizzasController as in Figure 5-7 and click Add again.

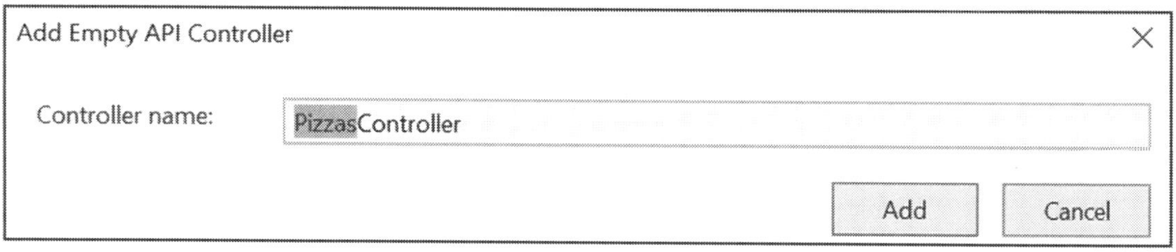

Figure 5-7. *Naming the controller*

If you are using Code, simply right-click the Controllers folder and select Add File. Name it PizzasController.cs.

This will add a new class called PizzasController, inheriting from ControllerBase, which you can see in Listing 5-3. Please note that the Route attribute indicates that the URI you should use is api/pizzas. The [controller] part of the route is a placeholder for the name of the controller, but without the Controller part.

Listing 5-3. The Empty PizzasController

```
namespace PizzaPlace.Server.Controllers
{
  [Route("api/[controller]")]
  [ApiController]
  public class PizzasController : ControllerBase
  {
  }
}
```

Let's add a method to retrieve a list of pizzas. For the moment you will hard-code the list, but in the next section you will retrieve it from a database. Modify the PizzasController as shown in Listing 5-4.

Listing 5-4. Adding a Method to the PizzaController to Retrieve a List of Pizzas

```
using System.Collections.Generic;
using System.Linq;
using Microsoft.AspNetCore.Mvc;
using PizzaPlace.Shared;
```

```
namespace PizzaPlace.Server.Controllers
{
  [ApiController]
  public class PizzasController : ControllerBase
  {
    private static List<Pizza> pizzas = new List<Pizza>
    {
      new Pizza(1, "Pepperoni", 8.99M, Spiciness.Spicy ),
      new Pizza(2, "Margarita", 7.99M, Spiciness.None ),
      new Pizza(3, "Diabolo", 9.99M, Spiciness.Hot )
    };

    [HttpGet("pizzas")]
    public IQueryable<Pizza> GetPizzas()
    {
      return pizzas.AsQueryable();
    }
  }
}
```

Let's walk through this implementation. First, you declare a hard-coded static list of pizzas. Next is the GetPizzas method, which has an attribute of HttpGet("pizzas"). This attribute says that when you perform a GET on the server with the pizzas URI the server should call the GetPizzas method.

The GetPizzas method returns an IQueryable<Pizza> and ASP.NET Core will send this result back to the client with the requested format. The IQueryable<Pizza> interface is used in .NET to represent data that can be queried, such as database data, and is returned by LINQ queries.

Note that the GetPizzas method contains nothing about HOW the data will be transferred to the client. This is all taken care of for you by ASP.NET Core! By default, your implementation in ASP.NET Core will use JSON, which is what you want.

Time to see if it works. First, ensure that the PizzaPlace.Server project is the startup project. Right-click the PizzaPlace.Server project and select Set as Startup Project from the drop-down menu. The PizzaPlace.Server project should be shown as bold, as in Figure 5-5.

Now run your project and wait for the browser to open because you will perform a GET; you can use the browser but for other verbs you will later use a nice tool called Postman.

Change the URI in the browser to http://localhost:xxxx/pizzas where xxxx is the original port number in your browser (the port number gets selected by Visual Studio and will be different than mine). You should see the result shown in Figure 5-8.

A JSON-encoded list of pizzas! It works!

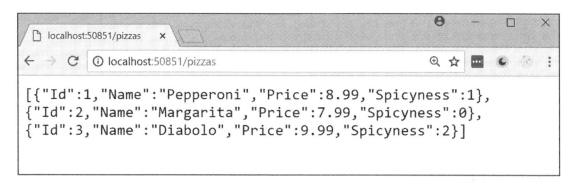

Figure 5-8. *The results of getting a list of pizzas from the pizza service*

Now you are ready to retrieve the data from a real database using Entity Framework Core.

What Is Entity Framework Core?

Entity Framework Core is the framework Microsoft recommends for working with databases. It allows you to write classes as normal C# classes and then store and retrieve .NET objects from a database without having to be an SQL expert. It will take care of this for you. This is also known as *persistence ignorance,* where your code does not need to know how and where data gets stored!

Using the Code First Approach

But of course, you need to explain to Entity Framework Core what kind of data you want to store. Entity Framework Core uses a technique called *code first*, where you write code to describe the data and how it should be stored in the database. Then, you can use this to generate the database, the tables and constraints. If you want to make changes to the database, you can update the database schema with *code first migrations*. If you already have a database, you can also generate the code from the database, but this is not the target of this book.

In the code first approach, you describe the classes (also known as entities) that will map to database tables. You already have the `Pizza` class (which you can find in the `PizzaPlace.Shared` project) to describe the Pizza table in the database. But you need to do more.

In this part you will be using SQL Server. If you installed Visual Studio on your Windows machine, SQL Server was installed too. If you don't have SQL Server on your machine, you can install a free version of SQL Server, or use a SQL Server instance in the cloud, for example SQL Server on Azure (`https://azure.microsoft.com/en-us/get-started/`).

You need to add Entity Framework Core to the `PizzaPlace.Server` project. If you are using Visual Studio, right-click the server project and select Manage NuGet Packages, as shown in Figure 5-9.

Figure 5-9. *Adding NuGet packages to your project*

The NuGet window will open in Visual Studio. NuGet is a very practical way for installing dependencies such as Entity Framework Core to your project. It will not only install the Microsoft.EntityFrameworkCore.SqlServer library, but also all its dependencies.

Select the Browse tab and type Microsoft.EntityFrameworkCore.SqlServer in the search box. You should see this library as the top search result. Select it, then select the Latest stable version from the Version drop-down, and click the Install button, as shown in Figure 5-10.

By the time you read this book, Microsoft might have deployed a more recent version, so although Figure 5-10 shows version 2.1.1, you should select the latest stable version.

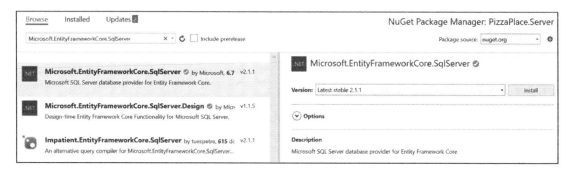

Figure 5-10. *Adding Entity Framework Core using NuGet*

With Code you open the command prompt and type in the following command after changing the current directory of your `PizzaPlace.Server` project:

```
dotnet add package Microsoft.EntityFrameworkCore.SqlServer
```

With this dependency installed you are ready to make some code changes. Entity Framework Core requires that entity classes have a default constructor and that properties are read-write. Update the `Pizza` class by adding a default constructor and adding setters for the properties, as shown in Listing 5-5.

Listing 5-5. Modifying the `Pizza` Class for Entity Framework Core

```
public class Pizza
{
  public Pizza() { }

  public Pizza(int id, string name,
               decimal price, Spiciness spicyness)
  {
    this.Id = id;
    this.Name = name ?? throw new ArgumentNullException(
                nameof(name), "A pizza needs a name!");
    this.Price = price;
    this.Spicyness = spicyness;
  }

  public int Id { get; set; }
  public string Name { get; set; }
  public decimal Price { get; set; }
  public Spiciness Spicyness { get; set; }
}
```

Add a new class called `PizzaPlaceDbContext` to the `PizzaPlace.Server` project, as shown in Listing 5-6. This class represents the database, and you do need to give a couple of hints about how you want your data to be stored in SQL Server (or some other database engine; this uses the same code).

Listing 5-6. The `PizzaPlaceDbContext` Class

```
using Microsoft.EntityFrameworkCore;
using PizzaPlace.Shared;

namespace PizzaPlace.Server
{
  public class PizzaPlaceDbContext : DbContext
  {
```

```
    public PizzaPlaceDbContext(
      DbContextOptions<PizzaPlaceDbContext> options)
      : base(options)
    { }

    public DbSet<Pizza> Pizzas { get; set; }

    protected override void OnModelCreating(
      ModelBuilder modelBuilder)
    {
      base.OnModelCreating(modelBuilder);

      var pizzaEntity = modelBuilder.Entity<Pizza>();
      pizzaEntity.HasKey(pizza => pizza.Id);
      pizzaEntity.Property(pizza => pizza.Price)
                 .HasColumnType("money");

    }
  }
}
```

First, you need to create a constructor for the PizzaPlaceDbContext class taking an DbContextOptions<PizzaPlaceDbContext> argument. This is used to pass the connection to the server, which you will do later in this section.

Next, you add a table to the database to represent your pizzas using a public property of type DbSet<Pizza>. DbSet<T> is the collection class used by Entity Framework Core, but you can think of it as a List<T>. Entity Framework Core will use the DbSet<T> to map this collection to a table, in this case the Pizzas table.

Finally, you override the OnModelCreating method, which takes a modelBuilder argument. In the OnModelCreating method, you can describe how each DbSet<T> should be mapped to the database; for example, you can tell it which table to use, how each column should be called, which type to use, etc. This modelBuilder has a bunch of methods that allow you to describe how the classes should be mapped to your database. In this case, you tell the modelBuilder that the Pizza table should have a primary key, the Id property of the Pizza class. You also need to tell how the Pizza.Price property should be mapped to SQL Server. You will use the SQL Server MONEY type for that. For the moment, this is enough for your current implementation.

Preparing Your Project for Code First Migrations

Now you are ready to tell the PizzaPlaze.Server project to use SQL Server as the database. You do this with dependency injection. In ASP.NET Core, you configure dependency injection in the Startup class' ConfigureServices method. Let's have a look at this method which is shown in Listing 5-7.

Listing 5-7. The Startup.ConfigureServices Method

```
public void ConfigureServices(IServiceCollection services)
{
  services.AddMvc().AddJsonOptions(options =>
  {
    options.SerializerSettings.ContractResolver =
      new DefaultContractResolver();
  });

  services.AddResponseCompression(options =>
  {
    options.MimeTypes = ResponseCompressionDefaults.MimeTypes
      .Concat(new[] {
        MediaTypeNames.Application.Octet,
        WasmMediaTypeNames.Application.Wasm,
      });
  });
}
```

Remember IServiceCollection from the chapter on dependency injection? Here dependencies for ASP.NET Core are added, such as dependencies for Mvc and ResponseCompression, which are required for your service.

Start by adding a constructor to the Startup class as in Listing 5-8.

Listing 5-8. The Startup Class' Constructor

```
using Microsoft.Extensions.Configuration;

...

public Startup(IConfiguration configuration)
```

```
{
  Configuration = configuration;
}

public IConfiguration Configuration { get; }
```

You need this constructor to have access to the projects configuration file. The configuration will contain the connection string for the database to talk to.

In the `ConfigureServices` you need to add any additional dependencies your implementation requires. Add the following code from Listing 5-9 at the end of the method.

Listing 5-9. Adding Entity Framework Dependencies

```
services.AddDbContext<PizzaPlaceDbContext>(options
  => options.UseSqlServer(
      Configuration.GetConnectionString("PizzaDb")));
```

This single statement tells ASP.NET Core that you will be using the `PizzaPlaceDbContext` and that you will be storing it in SQL Server. This code also looks up the connection string for the database in configuration, which you still need to add.

Right-click the `PizzaPlace.Server` project and select Add ➤ New Item. Type json in the search box and select App Settings File, as shown in Figure 5-11. Keep the default name of appsettings.json and click Add.

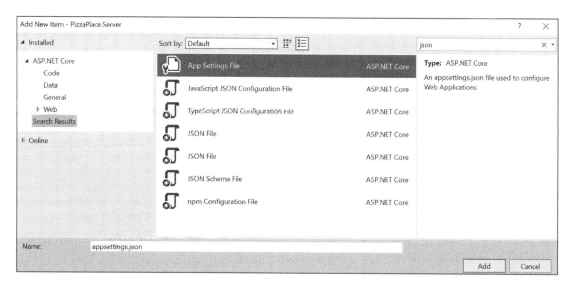

Figure 5-11. *Adding the application configuration file*

With Code, simply add a new file called `appsettings.json`. Double-click the new `appsettings.json` file to open it. ASP.NET Core uses a JSON file for configuration and you need to add a connection string to the database. A database connection string tells your code where to find the database server, which database to use, and which credentials should be used to log in. Visual Studio added a configuration file such as in Listing 5-10. This connection string uses the `(localdb)\\MSSQLLocalDB` server, which is the server installed with Visual Studio. The only things you need to do are to set the database name by replacing _CHANGE_ME into a more suitable name for your database and to change the name of the connection. Of course, if you are using another database server you will also have to change the server name too. Or read on to find out how to get the connection string with Visual Studio.

Listing 5-10. The `appsettings.json` Configuration File

```
{
  "ConnectionStrings": {
    "PizzaDb": "Server=(localdb)\\MSSQLLocalDB;Database=_CHANGE_ME;Trusted_
    Connection=True;MultipleActiveResultSets=true"
  }
}
```

Finding Your Database Server's Connection String

If you are not sure which connection string to use, you can find the connection string in Visual Studio by selecting View ➤ SQL Server Object Explorer.

You can connect to a database by clicking the server icon with the little green + sign, shown in Figure 5-12.

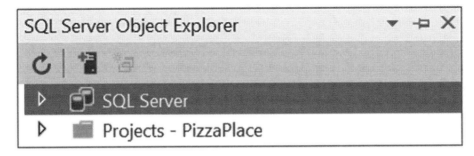

Figure 5-12. *SQL Server Object Explorer*

You can look for available database servers by expanding the Local, Network, or Azure as in Figure 5-13. I recommend that you try to find the MSSQLLocalDB database server. If you use another database server, you might need to change how to log in to your database. When you're ready, click Connect.

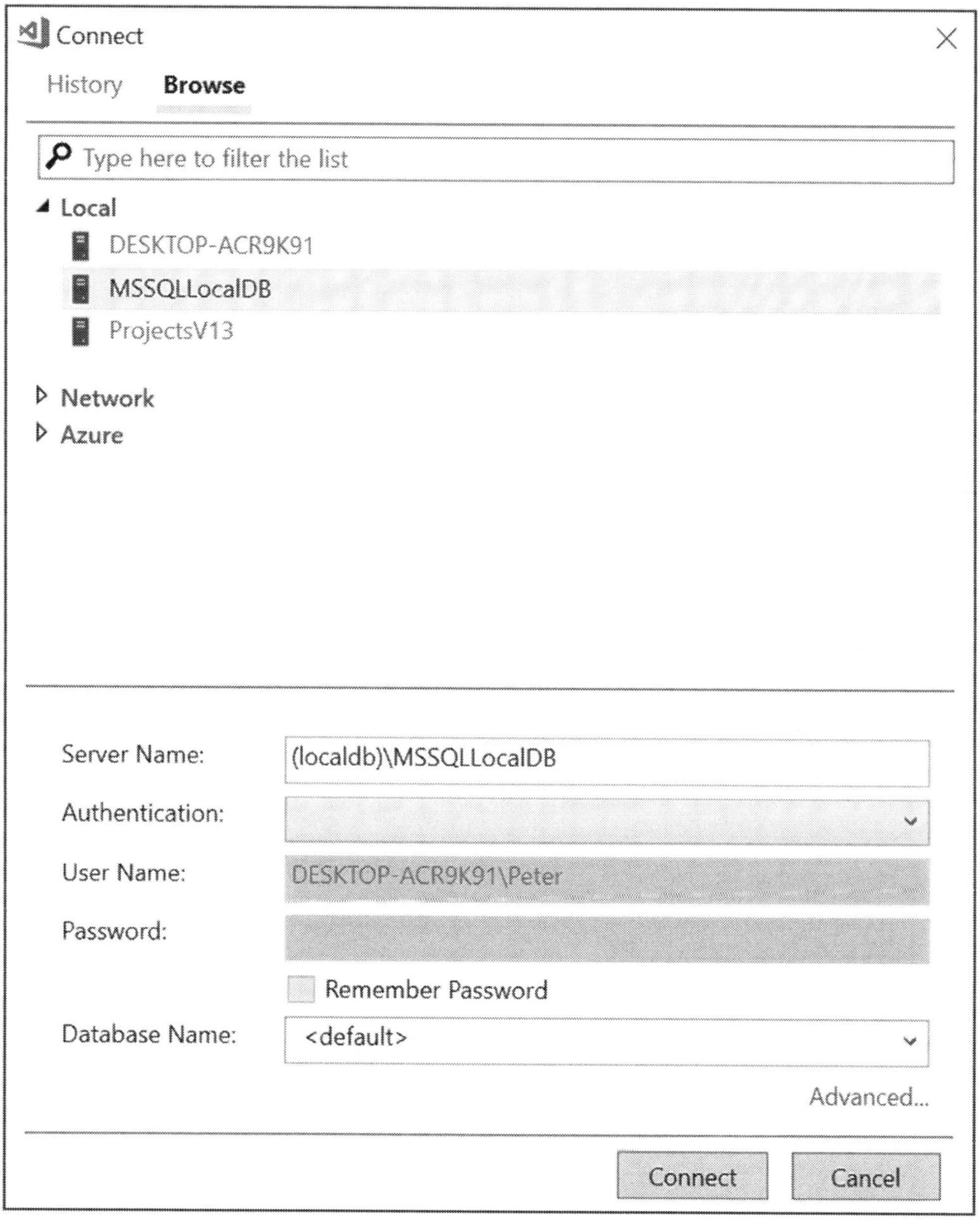

Figure 5-13. *Finding the connection string for a database*

Next, expand SQL Server from Figure 5-13 and select your server. Right-click it and select Properties. Now copy the connection string from the properties window and change the database name to `PizzaDb`.

Creating Your First Code First Migration

You are almost ready to generate the database from the code. But first you need to create a migration. A migration is a C# class that contains the changes that need to be made to the database to bring it up (or down) to the schema your application needs. This is done through a tool.

Start by selecting from the Visual Studio menu View ➤ Other Windows ➤ Package Manager Console, which you can see in Figure 5-14.

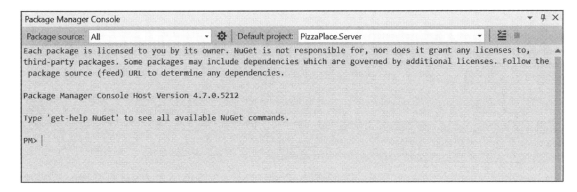

Figure 5-14. *The Package Manager Console*

Make sure that the default project is set to `PizzaPlace.Server`. This will make your commands target the selected project.

If you are using Code, use the integrated terminal or open a command prompt.

You must run the next command in the `PizzaPlace.Server` directory, so make sure you are in the correct directory. Optionally, type the following command to change the current directory to the `PizzaPlace.Server` project's directory:

```
cd PizzaPlace.Server
```

Now execute the following command to create the migration:

```
dotnet ef migrations add CreatingPizzaDb
```

Here you use the dotnet command to run the ef (Entity Framework) tool to add a new migration called CreatingPizzaDb. You should see following output (please ignore any differences in versions being shown):

```
info: Microsoft.EntityFrameworkCore.Infrastructure[10403]
      Entity Framework Core 2.1.0-rtm-30799 initialized
'PizzaPlaceDbContext' using provider 'Microsoft.EntityFrameworkCore.
SqlServer' with options: None
Done.  To undo this action, use 'ef migrations remove'
```

Should you get an error or warnings, please review the code for the Pizza and the PizzaPlaceDbContext classes and try again.

This tool created a new Migrations folder in the PizzaPlace.Server project with two files similar to Figure 5-15 but with a different timestamp.

Figure 5-15. *The result of adding the first migration*

Open the CreatingPizzaDb.cs file from Listing 5-11 and look what the tool did.

Listing 5-11. The CreatingPizzaDb.cs File

```
public partial class CreatingPizzaDb : Migration
{
  protected override void Up(
                        MigrationBuilder migrationBuilder)
  {
    migrationBuilder.CreateTable(
        name: "Pizzas",
        columns: table => new
        {
          Id = table.Column<int>(nullable: false)
          .Annotation("SqlServer:ValueGenerationStrategy",
```

```
            SqlServerValueGenerationStrategy.IdentityColumn),
            Name = table.Column<string>(nullable: true),
            Price = table.Column<decimal>(type: "money",
                                         nullable: false),
            Spiciness = table.Column<int>(nullable: false)
        },
        constraints: table =>
        {
            table.PrimaryKey("PK_Pizzas", x => x.Id);
        });
  }

  protected override void Down(
                    MigrationBuilder migrationBuilder)
  {
    migrationBuilder.DropTable(
        name: "Pizzas");
  }
}
```

A migration class has two methods: Up and Down. The Up method will upgrade the database schema. In this case, it will create a new table called Pizzas with Id, Name, Price, and Spiciness columns.

The Down method downgrades the database schema, in this case by dropping the column.

Generating the Database

Now you are ready to generate the database from your migrations. With Visual Studio, go back to the Package Manager Console window (View ➤ Other Windows ➤ Package Manager Console), or with Code open the integrated terminal (View ➤ Terminal) and type the following command:

```
dotnet ef database update --verbose
```

Because you asked the tool to be verbose this will generate a lot of output, among which you will find the DDL statements executed, such as in Listing 5-12.

Listing 5-12. An Extract from the Database Generation Tool's Output

```
CREATE TABLE [Pizzas] (
        [Id] int NOT NULL IDENTITY,
        [Name] nvarchar(max) NULL,
        [Price] money NOT NULL,
        [Spicyness] int NOT NULL,
        CONSTRAINT [PK_Pizzas] PRIMARY KEY ([Id])

);
```

This just created the database for you!

Let's have a look at the database. From Visual Studio, open View ➤ SQL Server Object Explorer and expand the tree for the PizzaDb database as in Figure 5-16 (on my system I have some other databases; just ignore them).

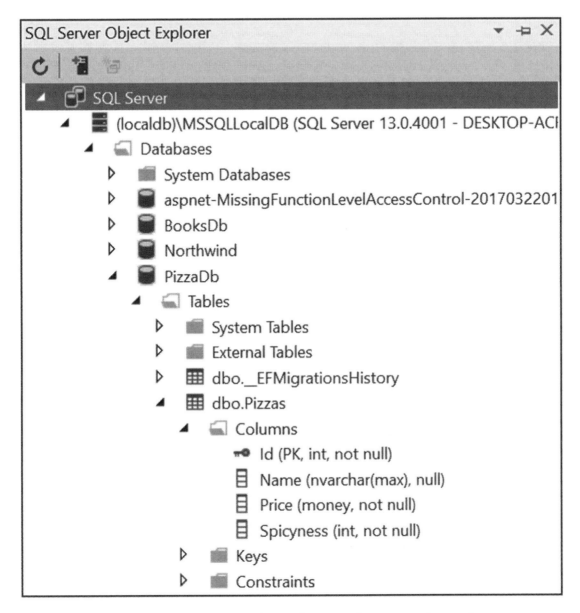

Figure 5-16. *SQL Server Object Explorer showing the PizzaDb Database*

If you don't have Visual Studio, you can download *SQL Operations Studio* from
`www.microsoft.com/en-us/sql-server/developer-tools`. After installation ends, SQL
Operations Studio will start. Enter your server name and select `PizzaDb` from the
drop-down list, as shown in Figure 5-17.

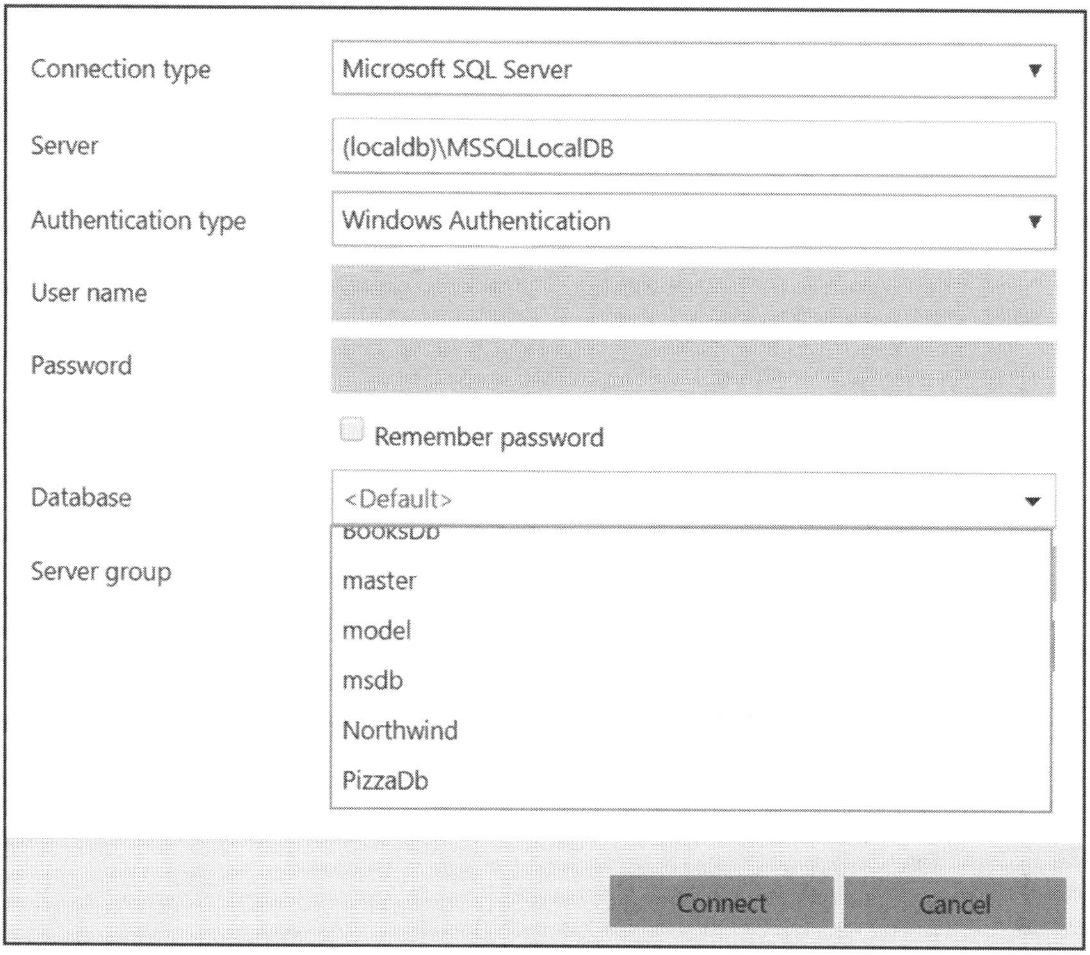

Connection type	Microsoft SQL Server	▼
Server	(localdb)\MSSQLLocalDB	
Authentication type	Windows Authentication	▼
User name		
Password		
	☐ Remember password	
Database	<Default>	▼
Server group	BOOKSDb	
	master	
	model	
	msdb	
	Northwind	
	PizzaDb	

Connect   Cancel

Figure 5-17.   Connection with SQL Operations Studio

Enhancing the Pizza Microservice

Let's add some functionality to the Pizza microservice so it uses the database instead of hard-coded data and add a method to insert a pizza in your database.

Open the `PizzaController` class, which sits in the `Controllers` folder of the `PizzaPlace.Server` project. Start by adding a constructor that takes the `PizzaPlaceDbContext` as an argument, as in Listing 5-13.

Listing 5-13. Injecting a `PizzaPlaceDbContext` Instance into the Controller

```
public class PizzasController : ControllerBase
{
  private PizzaPlaceDbContext db;

  public PizzasController(PizzaPlaceDbContext db)
  {
    this.db = db;
  }
```

To talk to the database, the `PizzasController` needs a `PizzaPlaceDbContext` instance, and as you learned in the chapter on *dependency injection*, you can use a constructor to do this. The constructor only needs to save the reference in a local field (for now).

You don't need the hardcoded list of pizzas, so remove the static field, and update the `GetPizza` method to use the `PizzaPlaceDbContext` instead, as in Listing 5-14. To get all the pizzas you can simply use the `Pizzas` property of the `PizzaPlaceDbContext`. The Entity Framework will access the database when it accesses the `Pizzas` property.

Listing 5-14. Retrieving the Pizzas from the Database

```
[HttpGet("pizzas")]
public IQueryable<Pizza> GetPizzas()
{
  return db.Pizzas;
}
```

Now let's add a method to insert a new pizza in the database. Add the `InsertPizza` method from Listing 5-15 to the `PizzasController` class. This method will receive a pizza instance from the client as part of the POST request body, so you add the `HttpPost` attribute with the URI that you should post to. The `pizza` object will be posted in the request body, and this is why the `InsertPizza` method's `pizza` argument has the `FromBody` attribute to tell ASP.NET MVC Core to convert the body to a pizza instance. The method adds the pizza to the `PizzaPlaceDbContext` `Pizzas` table and then saves it to the database. The `InsertPizza` method then returns a 201 Created status code with the URI of the pizza as the response. You will examine this response with Postman in the next part of this chapter.

Listing 5-15. The InsertPizza Method

```
[HttpPost("pizzas")]
public IActionResult InsertPizza([FromBody] Pizza pizza)
{
  db.Pizzas.Add(pizza);
  db.SaveChanges();
  return Created($"pizzas/{pizza.Id}", pizza);
}
```

This is an introduction to REST services. Building real services with all the different approaches and best practices can take up a whole book. The idea of this chapter is to get you up and running.

Testing Your Microservice Using Postman

So now you have your first microservice. But how do you test it? Previously you used to browser to test the GetPizzas method, but for other verbs you need a better tool. Here you will use Postman, which is a tool specifically for testing REST services.

Installing Postman

Open your favorite browser and go to www.getpostman.com. Download the application (click the Download the App button from Figure 5-18 and choose your platform) and install it.

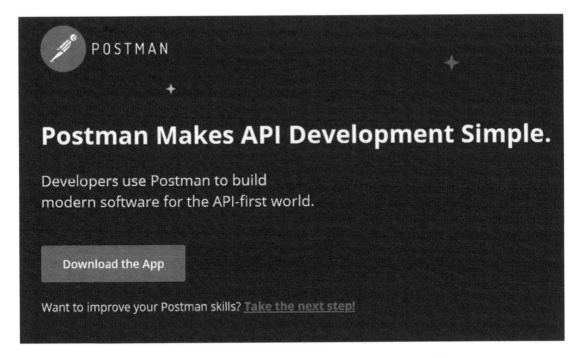

Figure 5-18. *The Postman web page*

By the time you read this book the installation procedure may have changed a bit, so please follow the instructions from the installer.

After it has installed, run Postman.

Making REST Calls with Postman

Postman will open, and it will ask you what you want to do. Select Request, as shown in Figure 5-19.

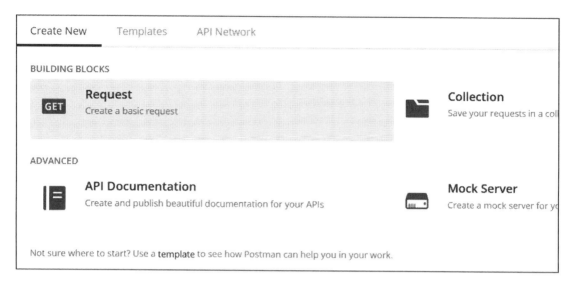

Figure 5-19. *Select Request to get started with Postman*

Then it will ask you where to save the request, so pick a name and a folder, as shown in Figure 5-20.

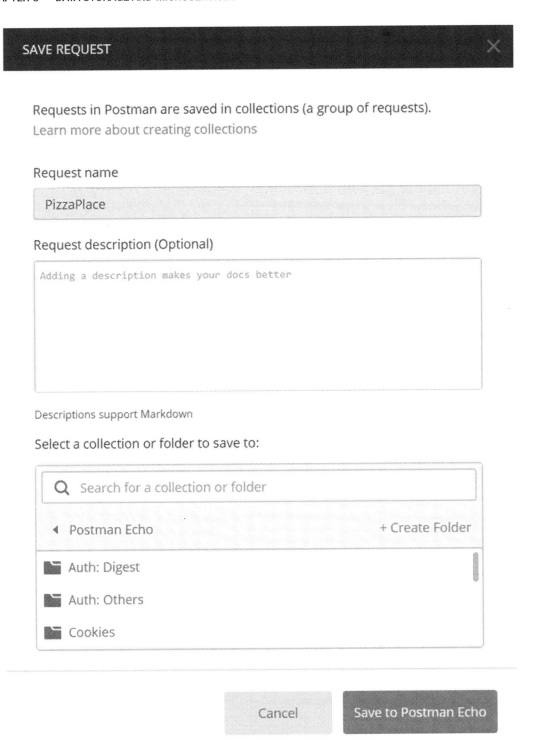

Figure 5-20. *Saving the request*

Making a GET Request

Now run the PizzaPlace solution and copy the URL from the browser. Paste it in Postman's "Enter the Request URL" field and append /`pizzas` as in Figure 5-21. Don't forget that you most likely will have a different port number!

Figure 5-21. *Making a GET request with Postman*

Before you click SEND, let's add the `Accept` header. Click the Headers tab and enter Accept as the key and application/json as the value. Please refer to Figure 5-22 for reference.

	GET ▾	http://localhost:50851/pizzas		Params

Authorization	Headers (1)	Body	Pre-request Script	Tests	

	Key	Value	Description
✅	Accept	application/json	
	New key	Value	Description

Figure 5-22. *Adding headers to the request in Postman*

Now you can click Send. You should receive an empty list as in Figure 5-23 (which is normal because you haven't added any rows to the pizza table yet).

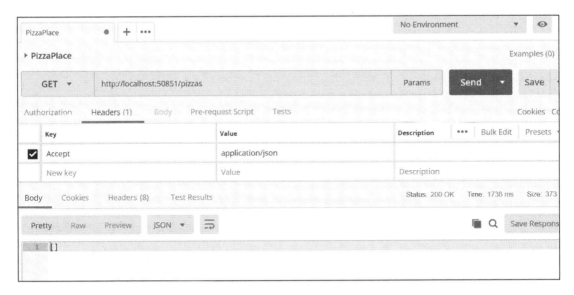

Figure 5-23. *Receiving an empty list of pizzas from the server*

Inserting Pizzas with POST

Let's add a couple of pizzas to the database. At the top of Postman, you will find a tab with a plus sign. Click it to add another tab. Select POST as the verb and copy the URI from the previous tab, as shown in Figure 5-24.

Figure 5-24. *Starting with the POST request*

Now select the Headers section and add a new header with key Content-Type and value application/json like in Figure 5-25.

Authorization	Headers (1)	Body ●	Pre-request Script	Tests

Key	Value
☑ Content-Type	application/json
New key	Value

Figure 5-25. *Adding the Content-Type header for the POST request*

Now select the Body section, click the raw format radio button, and enter a pizza object using JSON. Please refer to Figure 5-26. Note that this raw string contains the pizza's properties serialized as JSON, and that you don't need to send the Id property because the server will generate the id when it gets inserted into the database.

POST ▼   http://localhost:5000/pizzas

Authorization	Headers (1)	Body ●	Pre-request Script	Tests

● form-data   ● x-www-form-urlencoded   ● raw   ● binary   JSON (application/json) ▼

```
1 ▾ {
2       "Name":"Pepperoni",
3       "Price":8.99,
4       "Spiciness": 2
5   }
```

Figure 5-26. *Entering a pizza using JSON*

Click the Send button. If all is well, you should receive a positive 201 Created response. In the response area of Postman, select the Headers tab as in Figure 5-27. Look for the Location header. It will show the new URI given to this pizza. This Location header is returned by the Created method you called as the last line of Listing 5-15.

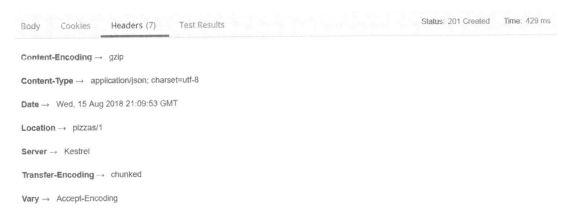

Figure 5-27. *The POST response in Postman*

Click the first tab where you created the GET request and click Send again. Now you should have a list of pizzas (a list of one). Try creating a couple of other pizzas. Figure 5-28 is my result after adding three pizzas.

```
 1 ▾ [
 2 ▾     {
 3             "Id": 1,
 4             "Name": "Pepperoni",
 5             "Price": 8.99,
 6             "Spicyness": 2
 7       },
 8 ▾     {
 9             "Id": 2,
10             "Name": "Margarita",
11             "Price": 7.99,
12             "Spicyness": 0
13       },
14 ▾     {
15             "Id": 3,
16             "Name": "Diabolo",
17             "Price": 9.99,
18             "Spicyness": 2
19       }
20   ]
```

Figure 5-28. *A list of pizzas stored in the database*

Summary

In this chapter, you had a look at how to store data on the server using Entity Framework Core and how to expose that data using REST and microservices. You added a pizza service to the PizzaPlace application and then went on testing it with Postman.

CHAPTER 6

Communication with Microservices

In the previous chapter, you build a microservice using ASP.NET Core and Entity Framework Core to retrieve the menu of pizzas from the server. In this chapter, you will add support to the Blazor client to talk to that microservice. You will also complete the project by adding support for completing the order.

Using the HttpClient Class

Start by opening the MyFirstBlazor solution you created in the first chapter. You will use this project to examine the template that was created for you. You will start by looking at the server side of the solution, then the shared project's code, and then the client side.

Examining the Server Project

Look at the MyFirstBlazor.Server project and look for the SampleDataController class, which is in Listing 6-1.

Listing 6-1. The SampleDataController Class

```
using MyFirstBlazor.Shared;
using Microsoft.AspNetCore.Mvc;
using System;
using System.Collections.Generic;
using System.Linq;
using System.Threading.Tasks;
namespace MyFirstBlazor.Server.Controllers
```

© Peter Himschoot 2019
P. Himschoot, *Blazor Revealed*, https://doi.org/10.1007/978-1-4842-4343-5_6

```
{
  [Route("api/[controller]")]
  public class SampleDataController : Controller
  {
    private static string[] Summaries = new[]
    {
        "Freezing", "Bracing", "Chilly", "Cool", "Mild",
        "Warm", "Balmy", "Hot", "Sweltering", "Scorching"
    };
    [HttpGet("[action]")]
    public IEnumerable<WeatherForecast> WeatherForecasts()
    {
      var rng = new Random();
      return Enumerable.Range(1, 5)
                     .Select(index => new WeatherForecast
      {
        Date = DateTime.Now.AddDays(index),
        TemperatureC = rng.Next(-20, 55),
        Summary = Summaries[rng.Next(Summaries.Length)]
      });
    }
  }
}
```

The SampleDataController class exposes one REST endpoint at /api/SampleData/
WeatherForecasts to retrieve a list of WeatherForecast objects. This time the
SampleDataController uses the [Route("api/[controller]")] attribute to set up the
endpoint to generically listen to an URI that contains the name of the controller (without
the suffix "Controller") and then uses the [HttpGet("[action]")] attribute to expect the
method name as the third part of the URI.

To invoke this method, you should use a GET on the api/SampleData/
WeatherForecasts URI, which you can try with your browser (or if you prefer, Postman).
Run the solution and type the URI in your browser (don't forget you will have a different
port number) which will result in Figure 6-1 (expect different weather).

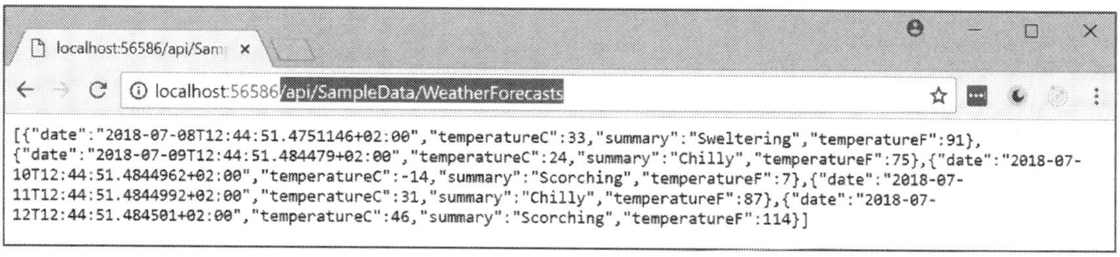

Figure 6-1. Invoking the service using the browser

The WeatherForecasts method from Listing 6-1 uses a random choice of temperatures and summaries to generate these forecasts, which is great for a demo.

Why Use a Shared Project?

Now open the WeatherForecast class from the MyFirstBlazor.Shared project, which is in Listing 6-2.

Listing 6-2. The Shared WeatherForecast Class

```
using System;

namespace MyFirstBlazor.Shared
{
  public class WeatherForecast
  {
    public DateTime Date { get; set; }
    public int TemperatureC { get; set; }
    public string Summary { get; set; }
    public int TemperatureF
    => 32 + (int)(TemperatureC / 0.5556);
  }
}
```

This WeatherForecast class is straightforward, containing the Date of the forecast, the temperature in Celsius and Fahrenheit, and a Summary, but I want to draw your attention to the fact that this class lives in the Shared project. This shared project is used both by the server and the client project.

If you ever created a web app with JavaScript you should be familiar with the experience of building a class for the server project, for example in C#, and building another class in JavaScript (or Typescript) for the client. You must make sure that both classes serialize to the same JSON format; otherwise you will get runtime errors, or even worse, lose data! If the model grows, you must update both classes again. This is a HUGE maintenance problem in these kinds of projects, because you run the risk of updating only one side on a busy workday.

With Blazor, you don't suffer from this because both server and client use C#. And that is why there is a Shared project. You put your classes here and they are shared between the server and client, and then you use them by simply adding a reference to the Shared project. Adding another piece of data means updating a shared class, which works easily! No longer must you update two pieces of code.

Looking at the Client Project

Now look at the `MyFirstBlazor.Client` project. Inside the `Pages` folder you will find the `FetchData` component from Listing 6-3.

Listing 6-3. The `FetchData` Component

```
@using MyFirstBlazor.Shared
@page "/fetchdata"
@inject HttpClient Http

<h1>Weather forecast</h1>

<p>This component demonstrates fetching data from the server.</p>

@if (forecasts == null)
{
<p><em>Loading...</em></p>
}
else
{
<table class="table">
  <thead>
    <tr>
      <th>Date</th>
```

```
      <th>Temp.   (C)</th>
      <th>Temp.   (F)</th>
      <th>Summary</th>
    </tr>
  </thead>
  <tbody>
    @foreach (var forecast in forecasts)
    {
      <tr>
        <td>@forecast.Date.ToShortDateString()</td>
        <td>@forecast.TemperatureC</td>
        <td>@forecast.TemperatureF</td>
        <td>@forecast.Summary</td>
      </tr>
    }
  </tbody>
</table>
}
@functions {
WeatherForecast[] forecasts;
protected override async Task OnInitAsync()
{
  forecasts = await Http.GetJsonAsync<WeatherForecast[]>
                  ("api/SampleData/WeatherForecasts");
}
}
```

Let's look at this line by line. The first line in Listing 6-3 adds a Razor @using
statement for the Shared project's namespace to the component. You need this because
you use the WeatherForecast class from the Shared project. Just like in C#, you use
using statements in Razor to refer to classes from another namespace.

The second line adds the path for routing. You will look at routing in the next chapter.
For the moment you should know that when the URI is /fetchdata the FetchData
component will be shown in the browser.

On the third line you inject the HttpClient instance using the @inject syntax from Razor. The HttpClient class is the one you will use to talk to the server. You will learn about the HttpClient class in detail later in this chapter.

I do want to point out that you should never instantiate an instance of the HttpClient class yourself. Blazor sets up the HttpClient class in a special way, and if you create an instance yourself, it simply will not work as expected! Another reason not to create an instance yourself is that this is a dependency of the FetchData component and components should never create dependencies themselves!

A little lower down in Listing 6-3 you will find an @if statement. Because you fetch the data from the server using an asynchronous way, the forecasts field will initially hold a null reference. So, if the forecasts field has not been set, you tell the user to wait. If you have a slow network, you can see this happening. When you test your Blazor application on your own machine, the network is fast, but you can emulate a slow network using the browser (in this case using Google Chrome).

How to Emulate a Slow Network in Chrome

Start your Blazor project so the browser opens the home page. Now open the debugger tools from the browser (on Windows you do this by pressing F12) and select the Network tab as in Figure 6-2. On the right side, you should see a drop-down list that allows you to select which kind of network to emulate. Select Slow 3G.

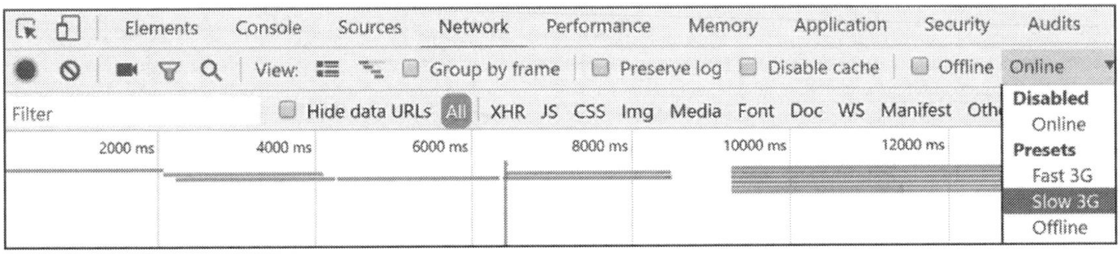

Figure 6-2. *Using the Chrome browser debugger to emulate a slow network*

Next, select the Fetch data tab on your Blazor site (should you already be on this tab, select another tab and then the Fetch data tab). Because you now are using a slow network the Loading... feedback will appear, as shown in Figure 6-3.

Weather forecast

This component demonstrates fetching data from the server.

Loading...

Figure 6-3. *The Loading... feedback with a slow network*

After testing your Blazor website with a slow network, don't forget to select Online from the drop-down from Figure 6-2 to restore your network to its normal speed.

If the forecasts field holds data, your Razor file will show a table with the forecasts by iterating over them, as you can see in the else part of Listing 6-3.

Onto the @functions section of the FetchData Razor file. First, you declare a field called forecasts to hold an array of WeatherForecast instances. Initially the forecasts field will hold a null value. You then override the OnInitAsync method. Blazor components have two methods that get called when the component has been initialized: OnInit and OnInitAsync. Because you fetch the data from the server using an asynchronous API you need to put your code in OnInitAsync. The OnInitAsync method is prefixed with C#'s async keyword, which makes it a breeze to call async APIs with the await keyword.

Asynchronous communication means that the client needs to wait a fair amount for the result to be returned. Instead of using a call that will stop Blazor from completing other request (freezing the user interface), you use the OnInitAsync method, which will wait in the background for the result.

You use the `Http.GetJsonAsync<WeatherForecast[]>("SOME URI")` to invoke the server's GET endpoint at the URI and you tell the `GetJsonAsync` method (using generics) to expect an array of `WeatherForecast` objects. When the result comes back from the server, you put the result into the `forecasts` field and Blazor will take care of rerendering the UI with your new data, as shown in Figure 6-4.

Weather forecast

This component demonstrates fetching data from the server.

Date	Temp. (C)	Temp. (F)	Summary
07/08/2018	-15	6	Chilly
07/09/2018	53	127	Sweltering
07/10/2018	45	112	Freezing
07/11/2018	-12	11	Chilly
07/12/2018	-16	4	Freezing

Figure 6-4. *Displaying the* `WeatherForecast` *objects*

Understanding the HttpClient Class

All communication between the client and server passes through the `HttpClient` class. This is the same class other .NET frameworks use and its role is to make the HTTP request to the server and to expose the result from the server. It also allows you to exchange binary or other formatted data, but in Blazor we normally use JSON.

> Google has defined a more efficient protocol called protocol buffers, which is also supported by Blazor. If you need to send a lot of data, you might want to look at protocol buffers.

The HttpClientJsonExtensions Methods

To make it a lot easier to talk to JSON microservices, Blazor provides you with a bunch of handy extension methods that take care of converting between .NET objects and JSON, which you can find in the `HttpClientJsonExtensions` class. I advise you use these methods, so you don't have to worry about serializing and deserializing JSON.

GetJsonAsync

The GetJsonAsync extension method makes an asynchronous GET request to the specified URI. Its signature is in Listing 6-4.

Listing 6-4. The GetJsonAsync Extension Method Signature

```
public static Task<T> GetJsonAsync<T>(
                    this HttpClient httpClient,
                    string requestUri)
```

Because it is an extension method you call it as a normal instance method on the HttpClient class, as shown in Listing 6-5.

This is also true for the other extension methods.

Listing 6-5. Using the GetJsonAsync Extension Method

```
forecasts = await Http.GetJsonAsync<WeatherForecast[]>
                ("api/SampleData/WeatherForecasts");
```

GetJsonAsync<T> will expect the response to contain JSON as specified by the generic argument. For example, in Listing 6-5 it expects an array of WeatherForecast instances. You invoke the GetJsonAsync method by prefixing it with the await keyword, which makes it asynchronous. Don't forget that you can only use the await keyword in methods and lambda functions that are async.

You can always inspect the request and response using your browser's debugger. Run your Blazor project and open the browser's debugger on the Network tab. Now select the Fetch data tab in your Blazor web site to make it load the data and look at the browser's Network tab, as shown in Figure 6-5.

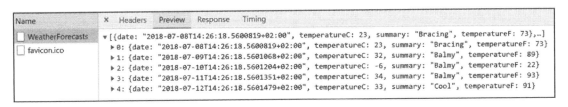

Figure 6-5. Inspecting the network using the browser's debugger

You can always clear the Network tab from previous requests before making the request using the clear button, which in Chrome looks like a circle with a slash through it (the forbidden sign).

See the `WeatherForecasts` entry in Figure 6-5? Now you can click that entry to look at the request and response. Let's start with the request preview shown in Figure 6-6.

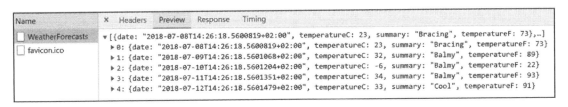

Figure 6-6. Using the Preview tab to look at the response

Using the Preview tab, you can see the server's response.

If you want to look at the request and response headers you can click the Headers tab, as shown in Figure 6-7.

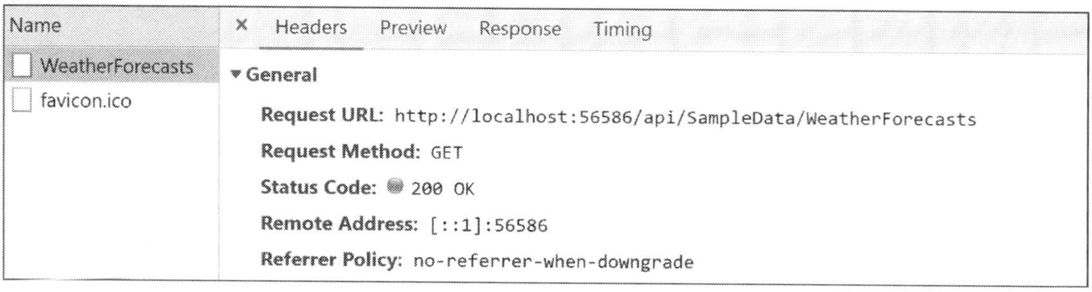

Figure 6-7. *Using the Headers tab to look at the request and the request/response headers*

Here you can see the request's URL and GET verb (the request method). It also shows the HTTP status code 200 OK. Scroll down to look at the headers. One of the response headers is Content-Type with a value of application/json, which was set by the server telling the client to expect JSON.

PostJsonAsync

The `PostJsonAsync` extension method makes a POST request with the content argument serialized in the request body as JSON to the specified URI. Its signature is in Listing 6-6.

Listing 6-6. The `PostJsonAsync` Method's Signature

```
public static Task PostJsonAsync(this HttpClient httpClient,
                            string requestUri,
                            object content)
```

You use this method if you don't expect any data back from the server. There is also a generic version of this method which expects a JSON response. Its signature is in Listing 6-7. This method will take the JSON response and deserialize it as a T.

Listing 6-7. The `PostJsonAsync<T>` Method's Signature

```
public static Task<T> PostJsonAsync<T>(
                this HttpClient httpClient,
                string requestUri,
                object content)
```

PutJsonAsync

The PutJsonAsync extension method makes a PUT request with the content argument serialized as JSON in the request body to the specified URI. Its signature is in Listing 6-8. Its usage is very similar to PostJsonAsync; the only difference is that it uses the PUT verb.

Listing 6-8. The PutJsonAsync Method's Signature

```
public static Task PutJsonAsync(this HttpClient httpClient,
                            string requestUri,
                            object content)
```

You use this method if you don't expect any data back from the server. There is also a generic version of this method which expects a JSON response. Its signature is in Listing 6-9. This method will take the JSON response and deserialize it as a T.

Listing 6-9. The PutJsonAsync<T> Method's Signature

```
public static Task<T> PutJsonAsync<T>(
                        this HttpClient httpClient,
                        string requestUri,
                        object content)
```

SendJsonAsync

With SendJsonAsync you can use any other verb that HTTP supports for making a request. Its signature is in Listing 6-10. The idea is that you pass the verb as the method parameter.

Listing 6-10. The SendJsonAsync Method's Signature

```
public static Task SendJsonAsync(this HttpClient httpClient,
                            HttpMethod method,
                            string requestUri,
                            object content)
```

You use this method if you don't expect any data back from the server. There is also a generic version of this method which expects a JSON response. Its signature is in Listing 6-11. This method will take the JSON response and deserialize it as a T.

Listing 6-11. The SendJsonAsync<T> Method's Signature

```
public static Task<T> SendJsonAsync<T>(
                        this HttpClient httpClient,
                        HttpMethod method,
                        string requestUri,
                        object content)
```

Retrieving Data from the Server

So now you are ready to implement the services you introduced earlier. Open the
PizzaPlace solution and look in the Blazor.Client project for Startup.cs, which is
shown in Listing 6-12.

Listing 6-12. Your Blazor Project's Startup Class

```
using Microsoft.AspNetCore.Blazor.Builder;
using Microsoft.Extensions.DependencyInjection;
using PizzaPlace.Shared;
namespace PizzaPlace.Client
{
  public class Startup
  {
    public void ConfigureServices(IServiceCollection services)
    {
      services.AddTransient<IMenuService,
                        HardCodedMenuService>();
      services.AddTransient<IOrderService,
                        ConsoleOrderService>();
    }
    public void Configure(IBlazorApplicationBuilder app)
    {
      app.AddComponent<App>("app");
    }
  }
}
```

In the ConfigureServices method you added two services, HardCodedMenuService and ConsoleOrderService. Let's replace these fake implementations with real services that talk to the server.

With Visual Studio, right-click the PizzaPlace.Client project and select Add ➤ New Folder from the drop-down menu. With Code, right-click the PizzaPlace.Client project and select New Folder. Name this folder Services. Now add a new class to this folder called MenuService, which can be found in Listing 6-13.

Again, you are applying the principle of single responsibility where you encapsulate how you talk to the server in a service. This way you can easily replace this implementation with another one should the need occur.

Listing 6-13. The MenuService Class

```
using Microsoft.AspNetCore.Blazor;
using PizzaPlace.Shared;
using System.Linq;
using System.Net.Http;
using System.Threading.Tasks;
namespace PizzaPlace.Client.Services
{
  public class MenuService : IMenuService
  {
    private HttpClient httpClient;
    public MenuService(HttpClient httpClient)
    {
      this.httpClient = httpClient;
    }
    public async Task<Menu> GetMenu()
    {
      var pizzas =
        await httpClient.GetJsonAsync<Pizza[]>("/pizzas");
      return new Menu { Pizzas = pizzas.ToList() };
    }
  }
}
```

You start by adding a constructor to this class taking the MenuService's dependency on HttpClient, and you store it in a field named httpClient. Then you implement the IMenuService interface's GetMenu method where you talk to the server calling the GetJsonAsync on the server's /pizza endpoint. Note that the /pizza endpoint is relative to the site's base (<base href="/" />), which can be found in the index.html file. Because the MenuService service returns a menu, and not a list of pizzas, you wrap the list of pizzas you got from the server into a Menu object. That's it!

Using the Principle of Single Responsibility results in many small classes, which are easier to understand, maintain, and test.

You have the service; now you need to tell dependency injection to use the MenuService. In the Startup class's ConfigureServices method, replace it as shown in Listing 6-14.

Listing 6-14. Replacing the HardCodedMenuService with the MenuService

```
using Microsoft.AspNetCore.Blazor.Builder;
using Microsoft.Extensions.DependencyInjection;
using PizzaPlace.Client.Services;
using PizzaPlace.Shared;
namespace PizzaPlace.Client
{
  public class Startup
  {
    public void ConfigureServices(IServiceCollection services)
    {
      services.AddTransient<IMenuService, MenuService>();
      services.AddTransient<IOrderService,
                       ConsoleOrderService>();
    }
    public void Configure(IBlazorApplicationBuilder app)
    {
        app.AddComponent<App>("app");
    }
  }
}
```

Run your project. You should see the list of pizzas (retrieved from your database) as in Figure 6-8!

Pizza Place

Our selected list of pizzas

Pepperoni	8.99		Order
Margarita	7.99		Order
Diabolo	9.99		Order

Figure 6-8. *The PizzaPlace app showing the pizzas from the database*

You will probably first see an empty menu, especially on a slow network. This might confuse some customers so let's add some UI to tell the customer to wait a bit. Update `pizzalist.cshtml` to look like Listing 6-15.

Listing 6-15. Adding a Loading UI to the `PizzaList` Component

```
<h1>@Title</h1>

@if (Menu == null || Menu.Pizzas == null
                || Menu.Pizzas.Count == 0)
{
  <div style="height:20vh;" class="pt-3">
    <div class="mx-left pt-3" style="width:200px">
      <div class="progress">
        <div class="progress-bar bg-danger
                    progress-bar-striped
                    progress-bar-animated w-100"
            role="progressbar"
            aria-valuenow="100" aria-valuemin="0"
            aria-valuemax="100"></div>
      </div>
    </div>
```

```
      </div>
}
else
{
  @foreach (var pizza in Menu.Pizzas)
  {
    <PizzaItem Pizza="@pizza" ButtonTitle="Order"
      ButtonClass="btn btn-success" Selected="@((p) => Selected(p))" />
  }
}

@functions {

[Parameter]
protected string Title { get; set; }
[Parameter]
protected Menu Menu { get; set; }
[Parameter]
protected Action<Pizza> Selected { get; set; }
}
```

If the menu has not been loaded yet, it will display a progress bar like in Figure 6-9.

Our selected list of pizzas

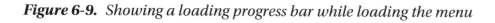

Figure 6-9. *Showing a loading progress bar while loading the menu*

Storing Changes

Now onto storing the order from the customer. Because you don't have a microservice yet for storing the order, you will build this first, and then you will implement the client service to send the order to the server.

Updating the Database with Orders

What is an order? Every customer has an order, and each order has one or more pizzas. A pizza can belong to more than one order, which can result in a specific problem: you need a many-to-many relation between pizzas and orders. In relational databases, this is done by adding a table between orders and pizzas, which you will map using a PizzaOrder class, as shown in Figure 6-10.

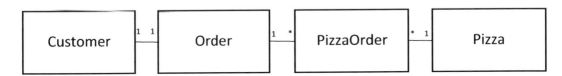

Figure 6-10. *Modelling the relationships*

Entity Framework Core 2.1 does not have support for hiding this extra table, so you need to do this manually. In future versions Microsoft will (hopefully) add this feature.

Add a new class to the PizzaPlace.Shared project called PizzaOrder, as shown in Listing 6-16.

Listing 6-16. The PizzaOrder Class

```
namespace PizzaPlace.Shared
{
  public class PizzaOrder
  {
    public int Id { get; set; }
    public Order Order { get; set; }
    public Pizza Pizza { get; set; }
  }
}
```

Next, add a new class named Order to the PizzaPlace.Shared project, as shown in Listing 6-17.

Listing 6-17. The Order Class

```
using System.Collections.Generic;

namespace PizzaPlace.Shared
{
  public class Order
  {
    public int Id { get; set; }

    public Customer Customer { get; set; }

    public int CustomerId { get; set; }

    public List<PizzaOrder> PizzaOrders { get; set; }

    public decimal TotalPrice { get; set; }
  }
}
```

Update the Customer class from the PizzaPlace.Shared project by adding an Order to it, as in Listing 6-18.

Listing 6-18. The Customer Class

```
using System;
using System.Collections;
using System.ComponentModel;
using System.Runtime.CompilerServices;
namespace PizzaPlace.Shared
{
  public class Customer : INotifyDataErrorInfo,
                         INotifyPropertyChanged
  {
    public int Id { get; set; }

    private string name;

    public string Name
    {
```

179

```
        get { return name; }
        set { name = value; OnPropertyChanged(); }
    }

    private string street;

    public string Street
    {
        get { return street; }
        set { street = value; OnPropertyChanged(); }
    }

    private string city;

    public string City
    {
        get { return city; }
        set { city = value; OnPropertyChanged(); }
    }

    public Order Order { get; set; }

  // The rest of the class omitted for clarity

}
```

And you need to add a new PizzaOrders property to the Pizza class as in Listing 6-19.

Listing 6-19. The Pizza Class

```
public class Pizza
{
  public Pizza() { }
  public Pizza(int id, string name, decimal price,
               Spiciness spicyness)
  {
    ...
  }
  public int Id { get; set; }
  public string Name { get; set; }
```

```
  public decimal Price { get; set; }
  public Spiciness Spicyness { get; set; }
  public List<PizzaOrder> PizzaOrders { get; set; }
}
```

Now you can add these tables to the PizzaPlaceDbContext class, which can be found in Listing 6-20.

Listing 6-20. The Updated PizzaPlaceDbContext Class

```
using Microsoft.EntityFrameworkCore;
using PizzaPlace.Shared;
namespace PizzaPlace.Server
{
  public class PizzaPlaceDbContext : DbContext
  {
    public PizzaPlaceDbContext(
      DbContextOptions<PizzaPlaceDbContext> options)
      : base(options)
    { }

    public DbSet<Pizza> Pizzas { get; set; }

    public DbSet<Customer> Customers { get; set; }

    public DbSet<Order> Orders { get; set; }

    public DbSet<PizzaOrder> PizzaOrders { get; set; }

    protected override void OnModelCreating(
                             ModelBuilder modelBuilder)
    {
      base.OnModelCreating(modelBuilder);
      var pizzaEntity = modelBuilder.Entity<Pizza>();
      pizzaEntity.HasKey(pizza => pizza.Id);
      pizzaEntity.Property(pizza => pizza.Price)
                 .HasColumnType("money");
```

```
        var customerEntity = modelBuilder.Entity<Customer>();
        customerEntity.HasKey(customer => customer.Id);
        customerEntity.HasOne(customer => customer.Order)
                    .WithOne(order => order.Customer)
                    .HasForeignKey<Order>(
                        order => order.CustomerId);
        var orderEntity = modelBuilder.Entity<Order>();
        orderEntity.HasKey(order => order.Id);
        orderEntity.HasMany(order => order.PizzaOrders)
                .WithOne(pizzaOrder => pizzaOrder.Order);
        pizzaEntity.HasMany(pizza => pizza.PizzaOrders)
                .WithOne(pizzaOrder => pizzaOrder.Pizza);
    }
  }
}
```

Here you have added the Customers, Orders and PizzaOrders tables, and in the OnModelCreating method you explain to Entity Framework Core how things should be mapped.

A Customer has a primary key Id and a one-to-one relation with an Order. When using a one-to-one relation, Entity Framework Core needs to know which side is the *master* in the relation, and that is why you need to add a foreign key to the Order class with the HasForeighKey<Order> method.

An Order has a primary key Id, and it has a many-to-one relationship with a PizzaOrder (one Order can have many PizzaOrders, and each PizzaOrder belongs to one Order).

Finally, you indicate that a Pizza can belong to many PizzaOrders, and a PizzaOrder has one Pizza. This way every Order can have many Pizza instances, and every Pizza can have many Order instances.

Build your project and fix any compiler error(s) you might have.

Now it is time to create another migration. This migration will update your database with your new tables. In Visual Studio, open the Package Manager Console (which you can find via View ➤ Other Windows ➤ Package Manager Console). With Code, open the integrated terminal.

Change the directory to the PizzaPlace.Server project

Now type following command:

```
dotnet ef migrations add HandlingOrders
```

This will create a migration for your new database schema.

Apply the migration to your database by typing following command:

```
dotnet ef database update
```

This concludes the database part.

Building the Order Microservice

Time to build the microservice for taking orders. With Visual Studio, right-click the Controllers folder of the PizzaPlace.Server project and select New ➤ Controller. Select an Empty API Controller and name it OrdersController. With Code, right-click the Controllers folder of the PizzaPlace.Shared project and select New File, naming it OrdersController. This class can be found in Listing 6-21.

Listing 6-21. The OrdersController Class

```
using System.Collections.Generic;
using System.Linq;
using Microsoft.AspNetCore.Mvc;
using PizzaPlace.Shared;

namespace PizzaPlace.Server.Controllers
{
  [ApiController]
  public class OrdersController : ControllerBase
  {
    private PizzaPlaceDbContext db;
    public OrdersController(PizzaPlaceDbContext db)
    {
      this.db = db;
    }
    [HttpPost("/orders")]
    public IActionResult CreateOrder([FromBody] Basket basket)
    {
```

```
        var customer = basket.Customer;
        var order = new Order() {
          PizzaOrders = new List<PizzaOrder>()
        };
        customer.Order = order;
        foreach (var pizzaId in basket.Orders)
        {
          var pizza = db.Pizzas.Single(p => p.Id == pizzaId);
          order.PizzaOrders.Add(new PizzaOrder {
            Pizza = pizza, Order = order
          });
        }
        order.TotalPrice =
          order.PizzaOrders.Sum(po => po.Pizza.Price);
        db.Customers.Add(customer);
        db.SaveChanges();
        return Ok();
      }
    }
}
```

Your `OrdersController` needs a `PizzaPlaceContextDb`, so you add a constructor taking the instance and you let dependency injection take care of the rest. To create a new order, you use the POST verb for the `CreateOrder` method taking a `Basket` instance in the request body. Upon receipt of a basket instance, you create the customer and order. You then set the customer's order. There is no need to set the order's `Customer` property; Entity Framework Core will take care of the inverse relationship for you. Next, you fill up the order's `PizzaOrders` collection with pizzas. Then you calculate the total price for the order and you save the whole Customer ➤ Order ➤ PizzaOrders ➤ Pizza chain by adding the root entity `Customer` to `PizzaPlaceDbContext` and calling SaveChanges. That's it. Entity Framework Core does all the work of storing the data!

Talking to the Order Microservice

Add a new class called `OrderService` to the `Services` folder of the `PizzaPlace.Client` project. This `OrderService` uses a POST request to the server, as shown in Listing 6-22.

Listing 6-22. The OrderService Class

```
using PizzaPlace.Shared;
using System.Threading.Tasks;
using Microsoft.AspNetCore.Blazor;
using System.Net.Http;

namespace PizzaPlace.Client.Services
{
  public class OrderService : IOrderService
  {
    private HttpClient httpClient;
    public OrderService( HttpClient httpClient)
    {
      this.httpClient = httpClient;
    }
    public async Task PlaceOrder(Basket basket)
    {
      await httpClient.PostJsonAsync("/orders", basket);
    }
  }
}
```

First, you add a constructor to the OrderService class, taking the HttpClient dependency, which you store in the httpClient field of the OrderService class. Next, you implement the IOrderService interface by adding the PlaceOrder method, taking a Basket as a parameter. Finally, you invoke the asynchronous PostJsonAsync method using the await keyword.

Now open the Startup class from the PizzaPlace.Client project and replace the ConsoleOrderService class with your new OrderService class, as shown in Listing 6-23.

Listing 6-23. Configuring Dependency Injection to Use the OrderService Class

```
using Microsoft.AspNetCore.Blazor.Builder;
using Microsoft.Extensions.DependencyInjection;
using PizzaPlace.Client.Services;
using PizzaPlace.Shared;
namespace PizzaPlace.Client
```

```
{
  public class Startup
  {
    public void ConfigureServices(IServiceCollection services)
    {
      services.AddTransient<IMenuService, MenuService>();
      services.AddTransient<IOrderService, OrderService>();
    }
    public void Configure(IBlazorApplicationBuilder app)
    {
      app.AddComponent<App>("app");
    }
  }
}
```

Run your PizzaPlace application and place an order for a couple of pizzas. Now open SQL Server Object Explorer in Visual Studio (or SQL Operations Studio) and examine the Customers, Orders, and PizzaOrders tables. They should contain your new order.

Summary

In this chapter, you learned that in Blazor you talk to the server using the HttpClient class, calling the GetJsonAsync and PostJsonAsync extension methods. You also learned that you should encapsulate calling the server using a client-side service class so you can easily change the implementation by switching the service type using dependency injection.

CHAPTER 7

Single Page Applications and Routing

Blazor is a .NET framework you use for building single-page applications, just like you can use popular JavaScript frameworks such as Angular, React and VueJs. But what is a SPA? In this chapter, you will use routing to jump between different sections of a SPA and send data between different components.

What Is a Single Page Application?

In the beginning of the Web there were only static pages. A *static page* is a HTML file somewhere on the server that gets send back to the browser upon request. Later came the rise of dynamic pages. When a browser requests a *dynamic page*, the server runs a program to build the HTML in memory and sends the HTML back to the browser (this HTML never gets stored to disk; of course, the server can store the generated HTML in its cache for fast retrieval later). Dynamic pages are flexible in the way that the same code can generate thousands of different pages by retrieving data from a database and using it to construct the page. But there is still a usability problem. Every time your user clicks on a link, the server must generate the next page from scratch and send it to the browser for rendering. This results in a noticeable wait period and of course the browser rerenders the whole page.

Then web pages started to use JavaScript to retrieve parts of the page when the user interacts with the UI. One of the first examples of this technique was Microsoft's Outlook Web Application. This web application looks and feels like Outlook, a desktop application, with support for all user interactions you expect from a desktop application. Google's Gmail is another example. They are now known as *single-page applications*. With SPAs certain sections of the web page are replaced at runtime depending on the user's interaction. If you click an e-mail, the main section of the page is replaced by the e-mail's view. If you click your inbox, the main section gets replaced by a list of e-mails, etc.

© Peter Himschoot 2019
P. Himschoot, *Blazor Revealed*, https://doi.org/10.1007/978-1-4842-4343-5_7

A SPA is a web application that replaces certain parts of the UI without reloading the complete page. SPAs use JavaScript to implement this manipulation of the browser's control tree (also known as the DOM) and most of them consist of a fixed UI and a placeholder element where the contents gets overwritten depending on where the user clicks. One of the main advantages of using a SPA is that you can make a SPA state-full. This means that you can keep information loaded by the application in memory. You will look at an example in this chapter.

Using Layout Components

Let's start with the fixed part of a SPA. Every web application contains UI elements that you can find on every page, such as a header, footer, copyright, menu, etc. Copy-pasting these elements to every page would be a lot of work and would require updating every page if one of these elements needed to change. Developers don't like to do that so every framework for building web sites has had a solution of this. For example, ASP. NET WebForms uses master pages, ASP.NET MVC has layout pages. Blazor also has a mechanism for this called layout components.

Blazor Layout Components

Layout components are Blazor components. Anything you can do with a regular component you can do with a layout component, like dependency injection, data binding, and nesting other components. The only difference is that they must inherit from the `BlazorLayoutComponent` class.

The `BlazorLayoutComponent` class defines a `Body` property as in Listing 7-1.

Listing 7-1. The `BlazorLayoutComponent` Class

```
namespace Microsoft.AspNetCore.Blazor.Layouts
{
  public abstract class BlazorLayoutComponent
                      : BlazorComponent
  {
    protected BlazorLayoutComponent();
```

```
    [Parameter]
    protected RenderFragment Body { get; }
  }
}
```

As you can see from Listing 7-1, the BlazorLayoutComponent class inherits from the BlazorComponent class. This is why you can do the same things as with normal components. Let's look at an example. Open the MyFirstBlazor solution from previous chapters. Now look at the MainLayout.cshtml component in the MyFirstBlazor.Client's Shared folder, which you'll find in Listing 7-2.

Listing 7-2. MainLayout.cshtml

```
@inherits BlazorLayoutComponent

<div class="sidebar">
    <NavMenu />
</div>

<div class="main">
    <div class="top-row px-4">
        <a href="http://blazor.net" target="_blank"
            class="ml-md-auto">About</a>
    </div>

    <div class="content px-4">
        @Body
    </div>
</div>
```

On the first line the MainLayout component declares that it inherits from BlazorLayoutComponent. Then you see a sidebar and main <div> element, with the main element data-binding to the inherited Body property.

In Figure 7-1 you can see the sidebar on the left side (containing the links to the different components) and the main area on the right side with the @Body emphasized with a black rectangle (which I added to the figure). Clicking the Home, Counter, or Fetch Data link in the sidebar will replace the Body property with the selected component, updating the UI without reloading the whole page.

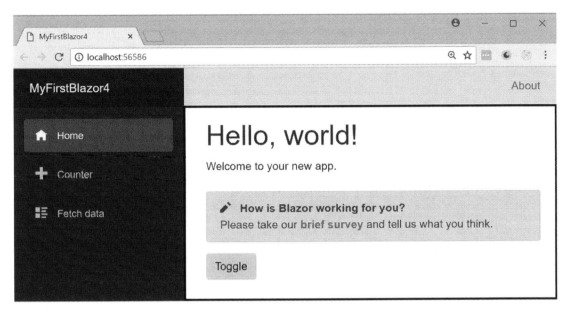

Figure 7-1. *The* `MainLayout` *component*

Selecting a @layout Component

Every component can select which layout to use by stating the name of the layout
component with the @layout directive. For example, start by copying the MainLayout.
cshtml file to MainLayout2.cshtml. This will generate a new layout component called
MainLayout2, inferred from the file name. Change the About link's text to Layout as in
Listing 7-3.

Listing 7-3. A Second Layout Component

```
@inherits BlazorLayoutComponent

<div class="sidebar">
    <NavMenu />
</div>

<div class="main">
    <div class="top-row px-4">
        <a href="http://blazor.net" target="_blank"
          class="ml-md-auto">Layout</a>
    </div>
```

190

```
    <div class="content px-4">
        @Body
    </div>
</div>
```

Now open the Counter component and add a @layout as in Listing 7-4.

Listing 7-4. Choosing a Different Layout with @layout

```
@page "/counter"
@layout MainLayout2

<h1>Counter</h1>

<p>Current count: @currentCount</p>

<button class="btn btn-primary" onclick="@IncrementCount">Click me</button>

@functions {
    int currentCount = 0;

    void IncrementCount()
    {
        currentCount++;
    }
}
```

Run the application and watch the layout change (the text of the link in the top right corner) as you alternate between Home and Counter.

You can also use the LayoutAttribute if you're building your component completely in code.

_ViewImports.cshtml

Most components will use the same layout. Instead of copying the same @layout directive to every page, you can also add a _ViewImports.cshtml file to the same folder as your components. Open the Pages folder from the MyFirstBlazor.Client project and look at the _ViewImports.cshtml file, which can be found in Listing 7-5.

Listing 7-5. `_ViewImports.cshtml`

```
@layout MainLayout
```

Any component that does not explicitly declare a `@layout` component will use the `MainLayout` component. Anything that is shared between all your components can be put in `_ViewImports.cshtml`, especially `@using` statements. A component can always override the `@layout` by explicitly adding the layout as in Listing 7-4.

Nested Layouts

Layout components can also be nested. You could define the `MainLayout` to contain all the UI that is shared between all components, and then define a nested layout to be used by a subset of these components. For example, add a new `Razor View` called `NestedLayout.cshtml` to the `Shared` folder and replace its contents with Listing 7-6.

Listing 7-6. A Simple Nested Layout

```
@inherits BlazorLayoutComponent
@layout MainLayout

<div class="container-fluid">
  <div class="row bg-primary text-white">
    <div class="col-sm-12">
      <h2>This is a nested layout</h2>
    </div>
  </div>
  <div class="row">
    <div class="col-sm-12">
      @Body
    </div>
  </div>
</div>
```

To build a nested layout you @inherit from BlazorLayoutComponent and set its @layout to another layout, for example MainLayout. Now make the Counter component use this nested layout as in Listing 7-7.

Listing 7-7. The Counter Component Is Using the Nested Layout.

```
@page "/counter"
@layout NestedLayout

<h1>Counter</h1>

<p>Current count: @currentCount</p>

<button class="btn btn-primary" onclick="@IncrementCount">Click me</button>

@functions {
int currentCount = 0;

void IncrementCount()
{
  currentCount++;
}

protected override void OnInit()
{
  base.OnInit();
}
}
```

Run your application and select the Counter component, as shown in Figure 7-2.

Figure 7-2. *The* Counter *component using the nested layout*

Understanding Routing

Single page applications use routing to select which component gets picked to fill in the layout component's Body property. Routing is the process of matching the browser's URI to a collection of *route templates* and is used to select the component to be shown on screen. That is why every component uses a @page directive to define the route template to tell the router which component to pick.

Installing the Router

When you create a Blazor solution from scratch the router is already installed but let's have a look at how this is done. Open App.cshtml. This App component only has one component, the Router component, as shown in Listing 7-8.

Listing 7-8. The App Component Containing the Router

```
<Router AppAssembly=typeof(Program).Assembly />
```

The router will look for all components that have the RouteAttribute (the @page directive gets compiled into a RouteAttribute) and pick the component that matches the current browser's URI. You will look at setting this RouteAttribute a little later in this chapter, but first you need to look at the NavMenu component.

The NavMenu Component

Review the MasterLayout component from Listing 7-2. On the fourth line you will
see the NavMenu component. This component contains the links to navigate between
components. Open the MyFirstBlazor solution and look for the NavMenu component in
the Shared folder, which is repeated in Listing 7-9.

Listing 7-9. The NavMenu Component

```
<div class="top-row pl-4 navbar navbar-dark">
  <a class="navbar-brand" href="">MyFirstBlazor</a>
  <button class="navbar-toggler" onclick=@ToggleNavMenu>
    <span class="navbar-toggler-icon"></span>
  </button>
</div>

<div class=@(collapseNavMenu ? "collapse" : null) onclick=@ToggleNavMenu>
  <ul class="nav flex-column">
    <li class="nav-item px-3">
      <NavLink class="nav-link" href=""
        Match=NavLinkMatch.All>
        <span class="oi oi-home" aria-hidden="true"></span>
        Home
      </NavLink>
    </li>
    <li class="nav-item px-3">
      <NavLink class="nav-link" href="counter">
        <span class="oi oi-plus" aria-hidden="true"></span>
        Counter
      </NavLink>
    </li>
    <li class="nav-item px-3">
      <NavLink class="nav-link" href="fetchdata">
        <span class="oi oi-list-rich"
              aria-hidden="true"></span>
        Fetch data
      </NavLink>
```

```
        </li>
      </ul>
</div>

@functions {
bool collapseNavMenu = true;

void ToggleNavMenu()
{
  collapseNavMenu = !collapseNavMenu;
}
}
```

The first part of Listing 7-9 contains a toggle button which allows you to hide and show the navigation menu. This button is only visible on displays with a narrow width (for example, mobile displays). If you want to look at it, run your application and make the browser width smaller until you see the *hamburger button* in the top right corner, as in Figure 7-3. Click the button to show the navigation menu and click it again to hide the menu again.

Figure 7-3. *Your application on a narrow display shows the toggle button*

The remaining markup contains the navigation menu, which consists of NavLink components. Let's look at the NavLink component.

The NavLink Component

The NavLink component is a specialized version of an anchor element <a/> used for creating navigation links. When the browser's URI matches the href property of the NavLink it applies a CSS style (the active CSS class if you want to customize it) to itself to let you know it is the current route. For example, look at Listing 7-10.

Listing 7-10. The Counter Route's NavLink

```
<NavLink class="nav-link" href="counter">
  <span class="oi oi-plus" aria-hidden="true"></span> Counter
</NavLink>
```

When the browser's URI ends with /counter (ignoring things like query strings) this NavLink will apply the active style. Let's look at another one in Listing 7-11.

Listing 7-11. The Default Route's NavLink

```
<NavLink class="nav-link" href="" Match=NavLinkMatch.All>
  <span class="oi oi-home" aria-hidden="true"></span> Home
</NavLink>
```

When the browser's URI is empty (except for the site's URL) the NavLink from Listing 7-11 will be active. But here you have a special case. Normally NavLink components only match the end of the URI. For example, /counter/55 matches the NavLink from Listing 7-10. But with an empty URI this would match everything! This is why in the special case of an empty URI you need to tell the NavLink to match the whole URI. You do this with the Match property, which by default is set to NavLinkMatch.Prefix. If you want to match the whole URI, use NavLinkMatch.All as in Listing 7-11.

Setting the Route Template

The Routing component from Blazor examines the browser's URI and searches for a component's route template to match. But how do you set a component's route template? Open the counter component shown in Listing 7-4. At the top of this file is the @page "/counter" directive. It defines the route template. A route template is a string that can contain parameters, which you can then use in your component.

Using Route Parameters

You can also specify parameters in the route template. By passing parameters in the route you can change what gets displayed in the component. You could pass the id of a product, look up the product's details with the id, and use it the display the product's details. Let's look at an example. Change the counter component to look like Listing 7-12.

Listing 7-12. Defining a Route Template with a Parameter

```
@page "/counter"
@page "/counter/{CurrentCount:int}"

@layout NestedLayout

<h1>Counter</h1>

<p>Current count: @CurrentCount</p>

<button class="btn btn-primary"
        onclick="@IncrementCount">Click me</button>

@functions {

  [Parameter]
  protected int CurrentCount { get; set; }

  void IncrementCount()
  {
      CurrentCount++;
  }
}
```

Listing 7-12 adds route template @page "/counter/{CurrentCount:int}". This tells the router component to match a URI like /counter/55 and to put the number in the CurrentCount parameter of your Counter component. You encase parameters in curly brackets. The Router component will put the value from the route in the property with the same name. You can also specify multiple parameters. Blazor does not allow you to specify default parameters, and this is why you need to specify two route templates. The first route template will pick the Counter component, with the CurrentCount set to its default value of 0. The second route template will pick the Counter component and set the CurrentCount parameter to an int value. It must be an int because of the int route constraint.

Filter URIs with Route Constraints

Just like routes in ASP.NET MVC Core you can use *route constrains* to limit the type of parameter to match. For example, if you were to use the /counter/Blazor URI, the route template would not match because the parameter does not hold an integer value and the router would not find any component to match.

Constraints are even mandatory if you're not using string parameters; otherwise the router does not cast the parameter to the proper type. You specify the constraint by appending it using a colon, for example "/counter/CurrentCount:int".

A list of other constraints can be found in Table 7-1.

Table 7-1. *Routing Constraints*

Route Constraints
Bool
Datetime
Decimal
Double
Float
Guid
Int
Long

If you are building your components as pure C# components, apply the RouteAttribute to your class with the route template as an argument. This is what the @page directive get compiled into.

Adding a Catchall Route Template

Most frameworks allow you to set a route template that catches all URIs that don't match any of the other route templates. For the moment Blazor does not support this, but the Blazor team is intent on adding this feature. Just be patient.

Redirecting to Other Pages

How do you navigate to another component using routing? You have three choices: use a standard anchor element, use the NavLink component, and use code. Let's start with the normal anchor tag.

Navigating Using an Anchor

Using an anchor (the <a/> element) is effortless if you use a relative href. For example, add Listing 7-13 below the button of Listing 7-12.

Listing 7-13. Navigation Using an Anchor Tag

```
<a class="btn btn-primary" href="/">Home</a>
```

This link has been styled as a button using Bootstrap 4. Run your application and navigate to the Counter component. Click the Home button to navigate to the Index component whose route template matches "/".

Navigating Using the NavLink Component

The NavLink component uses an underlying anchor, so its usage is similar. The only difference is that a NavLink component applies the active class when it matches the route. Generally, you only use a NavLink in the NavMenu component, but you are free to use it instead of anchors.

Navigating with Code

Navigating in code is also possible, but you will need an instance of the IUriHelper class through dependency injection. This instance allows you to examine the page's URI and has the helpful NavigateTo method. This method takes a string that will become the browser's new URI.

Let's try an example. Modify the counter component to look like Listing 7-14.

Listing 7-14. Using the IUriHelper

```
@using Microsoft.AspNetCore.Blazor.Services
@page "/counter"
@page "/counter/{CurrentCount:int}"
@layout NestedLayout
@inject IUriHelper uriHelper

<h1>Counter</h1>

<p>Current count: @CurrentCount</p>

<button class="btn btn-primary" onclick="@IncrementCount">Click me</button>
<a class="btn btn-primary" href="/">Home</a>
<button class="btn btn-primary"
        onclick="@StartFrom50">Start from 50</button>

@functions {

[Parameter]
protected int CurrentCount { get; set; }

void IncrementCount()
{
    CurrentCount++;
}

void StartFrom50()
{
    uriHelper.NavigateTo("/counter/50");
}
}
}
```

To use the IUriHelper you need to add a @using directive for the Microsoft. AspNetCore.Blazor.Services namespace. Then you tell dependency injection with the @inject directive to give you an instance of the IUriHelper and put it in the uriHelper field. Then you add a button that calls the StartFrom50 method when clicked. This method uses the uriHelper to navigate to another URI by calling the NavigateTo method. Run your application and click the "Start from 50" button. You should navigate to /counter/50.

Understanding the Base Tag

Please don't use absolute URIs when navigating. Why? Because when you deploy your application on the Internet the base URI will change. Instead Blazor uses the `<base/>` element and all relative URIs will be combined with this `<base/>` tag. Where is the `<base/>` tag? Open the `wwwroot` folder of your Blazor project and open `index.html`, shown in Listing 7-15.

Listing 7-15. `Index.html`

```
<!DOCTYPE html>
<html>
<head>
    <meta charset="utf-8" />
    <meta name="viewport" content="width=device-width">
    <title>MyFirstBlazor</title>
    <base href="/" />
    <link href="css/bootstrap/bootstrap.min.css"
        rel="stylesheet" />
    <link href="css/site.css" rel="stylesheet" />
</head>
<body>
    <app>Loading...</app>

    <script src="_framework/blazor.webassembly.js"></script>
</body>
</html>
```

When you deploy in production, all you need to do is to update the `base` tag. For example, you might deploy your application to `https://online.u2u.be/selfassessment`. In this case, you would update the base element to `<base href="/selfassessment" />`. So why do you need to do this? If you deploy to `https://online.u2u.be/selfassesment`, the counter component's URI becomes `https://online.u2u.be/selfassessment/counter`. Routing will ignore the base URI so it will match the counter as expected. You only need to specify the base URI once, as shown in Listing 7-15.

Sharing State Between Components

When you navigate between different Blazor components with routing you will probably encounter the need to send information from one component to another. One way to accomplish this is by setting a parameter in the destination component by passing it in the URI. For example, you could navigate to /pizzadetail/5 to tell the destination component to display information about the pizza with id 5. The destination component can then use a service to load the information about pizza #5 and then display this information. But in Blazor there is another way. You can build a State class (most developers call this State, but this is just a convention and you can call it anything you want; State just makes sense) and then use dependency injection to give every component the same instance of this class. This is also known as the Singleton Pattern. Your Pizza Place application is already using a State class, so it should not be too much work to use this pattern.

Start by opening the Pizza Place solution from previous chapters. Open the Index component from the Pages folder (in the PizzaPlace.Client project) and look for the private State field. Remove this field (I've made it a comment) and replace it with an @inject directive as in Listing 7-16.

Listing 7-16. Using Dependency Injection to Get the State Singleton Instance

```
@page "/"
@inject IMenuService  menuService
@inject IOrderService  orderService
@inject State State

<!-- Menu -->
<PizzaList Title="Our selected list of pizzas"
          Menu="@State.Menu"
          Selected="@((pizza) => AddToBasket(pizza))" />
<!-- End menu -->
<!-- Shopping Basket -->
<ShoppingBasket Title="Your current order"
              Basket="@State.Basket"
              GetPizzaFromId="@State.Menu.GetPizza"
              Selected="@(pos => RemoveFromBasket(pos))" />
<!-- End shopping basket -->
```

```
<!-- Customer entry -->
<CustomerEntry Title="Please enter your details below"
               bind-Customer="@State.Basket.Customer"
               Submit="@((_) => PlaceOrder())" />
<!-- End customer entry -->

<p>@State.ToJson()</p>

@functions {

//private State State { get; } = new State();

protected override async Task OnInitAsync()
{
  State.Menu = await menuService.GetMenu();
}

private void AddToBasket(Pizza pizza)
{
  Console.WriteLine($"Added pizza {pizza.Name}");
  State.Basket.Add(pizza.Id);
  StateHasChanged();
}

private void RemoveFromBasket(int pos)
{
  Console.WriteLine($"Removing pizza at pos {pos}");
  State.Basket.RemoveAt(pos);
  StateHasChanged();
}

private async Task PlaceOrder()
{
  await orderService.PlaceOrder(State.Basket);
}

}
```

Now configure dependency injection in Startup.cs to inject the State instance as a singleton, as in Listing 7-17.

Listing 7-17. Configuring Dependency Injection for the State Singleton

```
using Microsoft.AspNetCore.Blazor.Builder;
using Microsoft.Extensions.DependencyInjection;
using PizzaPlace.Client.Services;
using PizzaPlace.Shared;

namespace PizzaPlace.Client
{
  public class Startup
  {
    public void ConfigureServices(IServiceCollection services)
    {
      services.AddTransient<IMenuService, MenuService>();
      services.AddTransient<IOrderService, OrderService>();
      services.AddSingleton<State>();
    }

    public void Configure(IBlazorApplicationBuilder app)
    {
        app.AddComponent<App>("app");
    }
  }
}
```

Run the application. Everything should still work! What you've done is to use the *Singleton Pattern* to inject the State singleton into the Index component. Let's add another component that will use the same State instance.

You want to display more information about a pizza using a new component, but before you do this you need to update the State class. Add a new property called CurrentPizza to the State class, as shown in Listing 7-18.

Listing 7-18. Adding a CurrentPizza Property to the State Class

```
using System;
using System.Collections.Generic;
using System.Text;
using System.Linq;
```

205

```
namespace PizzaPlace.Shared
{
  public class State
  {
    public Menu Menu { get; set; } = new Menu();

    public Basket Basket { get; set; } = new Basket();

    public UI UI { get; set; } = new UI();

    public decimal TotalPrice
      => Basket.Orders.Sum(id => Menu.GetPizza(id).Price);

    public Pizza CurrentPizza { get; set; }
  }
}
```

Now when someone clicks on a pizza in the menu, it will display the pizza's information. Update the PizzaItem component by wrapping the pizza name in an anchor, like in Listing 7-19.

Listing 7-19. Adding an Anchor to Display the Pizza's Information

```
@using Microsoft.AspNetCore.Blazor.Services
@using PizzaPlace.Shared

<div class="row">
  <div class="col">
    <a href=""
       onclick="@(() => ShowPizzaInformation(Pizza))">
       @Pizza.Name</a>
  </div>
  <div class="col">
    @Pizza.Price
  </div>
  <div class="col">
    <img src="@SpicinessImage(Pizza.Spiciness)"
         alt="@Pizza.Spiciness" />
  </div>
```

```
<div class="col">
  <button class="@ButtonClass"
          onclick="@(() => Selected(Pizza))">
          @ButtonTitle</button>
  </div>
</div>

@functions {

  [Parameter]
  protected Pizza Pizza { get; set; }

  [Parameter]
  protected string ButtonTitle { get; set; }

  [Parameter]
  protected string ButtonClass { get; set; }

  [Parameter]
  protected Action<Pizza> Selected { get; set; }

  [Parameter]
  protected Action<Pizza> ShowPizzaInformation { get; set; }

  private string SpicinessImage(Spiciness spiciness)
  => $"images/{spiciness.ToString().ToLower()}.png";
}
```

When someone clicks this link, it will set the State instance's CurrentPizza property. But you don't have access to the State object. One way to solve this would be by injecting the State instance in the PizzaItem component. But you don't want to overburden this component, so you add a ShowPizzaInformation callback delegate to tell the containing PizzaList component that you want to display more information about the pizza. Clicking the pizza name link simply invokes this callback without knowing what should happen.

You are applying a pattern here known as "Dumb and Smart Components." A dumb component is a component that knows nothing about the global picture of the application. Because it doesn't know anything about the rest of the application a dumb component is easier to reuse. A smart component knows about the other parts of the application and will use dumb components to display its information. In your example the `PizzaList` and `PizzaItem` are dumb components, while the `Index` component is a smart component.

Update the `PizzaList` component to set the `PizzaItem` component's `ShowPizzaInformation` parameter as in Listing 7-20.

Listing 7-20. Adding a `PizzaInformation` Callback to the `PizzaList` Component

```
@using PizzaPlace.Shared

<h1>@Title</h1>

@if (Menu == null || Menu.Pizzas == null
     || Menu.Pizzas.Count == 0)
{
  <div style="height:20vh;" class="pt-3">
    <div class="mx-left pt-3" style="width:200px">
      <div class="progress">
        <div class="progress-bar bg-danger progress-bar-striped
        progress-bar-animated w-100" role="progressbar" aria-valuenow="100"
        aria-valuemin="0" aria-valuemax="100"></div>
      </div>
    </div>
  </div>
}
else
{
  @foreach (var pizza in Menu.Pizzas)
  {
    <PizzaItem Pizza="@pizza" ButtonTitle="Order"
```

```
            ButtonClass="btn btn-success"
            Selected="@((p) => Selected(p))"
            ShowPizzaInformation="@ShowPizzaInformation"/>
  }
}

@functions {

[Parameter]
protected string Title { get; set; }

[Parameter]
protected Menu Menu { get; set; }

[Parameter]
protected Action<Pizza> Selected { get; set; }

[Parameter]
protected Action<Pizza> ShowPizzaInformation { get; set; }

}
```

You added a ShowPizzaInformation callback to the PizzaList component and you simply pass it to the PizzaItem component. The Index component will set this callback and the PizzaList will pass it to the PizzaItem component.

Update the Index component to set the State instance's CurrentPizza and navigate to the PizzaInfo component, as shown in Listing 7-21.

Listing 7-21. The Index Component Navigates to the PizzaInfo Component

```
@page "/"
@using Microsoft.AspNetCore.Blazor.Services
@inject IMenuService   menuService
@inject IOrderService  orderService
@inject State State
@inject IUriHelper UriHelper

<!-- Menu -->
<PizzaList Title="Our selected list of pizzas"
           Menu="@State.Menu"
```

```
                Selected="@((pizza) => AddToBasket(pizza))"
                ShowPizzaInformation="@((pizza) => ShowPizzaInformation(pizza))"/>
<!-- End menu -->
<!-- Shopping Basket -->
<ShoppingBasket Title="Your current order"
                Basket="@State.Basket"
                GetPizzaFromId="@State.Menu.GetPizza"
                Selected="@(pos => RemoveFromBasket(pos))" />
<!-- End shopping basket -->
<!-- Customer entry -->
<CustomerEntry Title="Please enter your details below"
                bind-Customer="@State.Basket.Customer"
                Submit="@(async (_) => await PlaceOrder())" />
<!-- End customer entry -->

<p>@State.ToJson()</p>

@functions {

//private State State { get; } = new State();

protected override async Task OnInitAsync()
{
  State.Menu = await menuService.GetMenu();
}

private void AddToBasket(Pizza pizza)
{
  Console.WriteLine($"Added pizza {pizza.Name}");
  State.Basket.Add(pizza.Id);
  StateHasChanged();
}

private void RemoveFromBasket(int pos)
{
  Console.WriteLine($"Removing pizza at pos {pos}");
  State.Basket.RemoveAt(pos);
  StateHasChanged();
}
```

```
private async Task PlaceOrder()
{
  await orderService.PlaceOrder(State.Basket);
}

private void ShowPizzaInformation(Pizza pizza)
{
  State.CurrentPizza = pizza;
  UriHelper.NavigateTo("/PizzaInfo");
}

}
```

The Index component tells the PizzaList component to call the ShowPizzaInformation method when someone clicks the information link from the PizzaItem component. The ShowPizzaInformation method then sets the State's CurrentPizza property and navigates using the UriHelper.NavigateTo method to the /PizzaInfo route.

Right-click the Pages folder and add a new Razor View called PizzaInfo, as shown in Listing 7-22 (to save you some time and to keep things simple, you can copy most of the PizzaItem component). The PizzaInfo component shows information about the State's CurrentPizza. This works because you share the same State instance between these components.

Listing 7-22. Adding a PizzaInfo Component

```
@using PizzaPlace.Shared
@page "/PizzaInfo"
@inject State State

<h2>Pizza Details</h2>

<div class="row">
  <div class="col">
    @State.CurrentPizza.Name
  </div>
</div>
<div class="row">
  <div class="col">
    @State.CurrentPizza.Price
```

```
    </div>
  </div>
  <div class="row">
    <div class="col">
      <img src="@SpicinessImage(State.CurrentPizza.Spiciness)"
           alt="@State.CurrentPizza.Spiciness" />
    </div>
  </div>
  <div class="row">
    <div class="col">
      <a class="btn btn-primary" href="/">Menu</a>
    </div>
  </div>

@functions {

private string SpicinessImage(Spiciness spiciness)
=> $"images/{spiciness.ToString().ToLower()}.png";
}
```

At the bottom of the markup you add an anchor (and made it look like a button using Bootstrap styling) to return to the menu. It's an example of changing the route with anchors. Of course, in a real-life application you would show the ingredients of the pizza, a nice picture, and other information. I leave this as an exercise for you.

Summary

In this chapter, you looked at two things, layouts and routing.

Layouts allow you to avoid replicating markup in your application and help keep your application's look consistent. You also saw that layouts can be nested.

Routing is an important part of building single page applications and takes care of picking the component to show based on the browser's URI. You define route templates using the @page syntax where you use route parameters and constraints. Navigation in your single page application can be done using anchor tags and from code using the IUriHelper class. Then you modified the Pizza Place application to show how to share information between different routes in a Blazor application.

CHAPTER 8

JavaScript Interoperability

Sometimes there is just no escape from using JavaScript ☺. For example, Blazor itself uses JavaScript to update the browser's DOM from your Blazor components. You can, too. In this chapter, you will look at interoperability with JavaScript and, as an example, you will build a Blazor component library to display a line chart using a popular open-source JavaScript library for charts. This chapter does require you to have some basic JavaScript knowledge.

Calling JavaScript from C#

Browsers have a lot of capabilities you might want to use in your Blazor web site. For example, you might want to use the Browser's *local storage* to keep track of some data. Thanks to Blazor's JavaScript interoperability, this is easy.

Providing a Glue Function

To call JavaScript functionality you start by building a *glue function* in JavaScript. I like to call these functions glue functions (my own naming convention) because they become the glue between .NET and JavaScript.

Glue functions are regular JavaScript functions. A JavaScript glue function can take any number of arguments, on the condition that they are JSON serializable (meaning that you can only use types that are convertible to JSON, including classes whose properties are JSON serializable). This is required because the arguments and return type are sent as JSON between .NET and JavaScript runtimes.

You then add this function to the *global scope* object, which in the browser is the window object. You will look at an example a little later, so keep reading. You can then call this JavaScript glue function from your Blazor component, as you will see in the next section.

© Peter Himschoot 2019
P. Himschoot, *Blazor Revealed*, https://doi.org/10.1007/978-1-4842-4343-5_8

Using JSRuntime to Call the Glue Function

Back to .NET land. To invoke your JavaScript glue function from C#, you use the .NET IJSRuntime instance provided through the JSRuntime.Current static property. This instance has the InvokeAsync<T> generic method, which takes the name of the glue function and its arguments and returns a value of type T, which is the .NET return type of the glue function. If this sounds confusing, you will look at an example right away...

The InvokeAsync method is asynchronous to support all asynchronous scenarios, and this is the recommended way of calling JavaScript. If you need to call the glue function synchronously, you can downcast the IJSRuntime instance to IJSInProcessRuntime and call its synchronous Invoke<T> method. This method takes the same arguments as InvokeAsync<T> with the same constraints.

Storing Data in the Browser with Interop

It's time to look at an example and you will start with the JavaScript glue function. Open the MyFirstBlazor solution you used in previous chapters. Open the wwwroot folder from the MyFirstBlazor.Client project and add a new subfolder called scripts. Add a new JavaScript file to the scripts folder called interop.js and add the glue functions from Listing 8-1. These glue functions allow you to access the localStorage object from the browser, which allows you to store data on the client's computer so you can access it later, even after the user has restarted the browser.

Listing 8-1. The getProperty and setProperty Glue Functions

```
window.interop = {
  setProperty: function (name, value) {
    window.localStorage[name] = value;
    return value;
  },
  getProperty: function (name) {
    return window.localStorage[name];
  }
};
```

Your Blazor web site needs to include this script, so open the index.html file from the wwwroot folder and add a script reference after the Blazor script, as shown in Listing 8-2.

Listing 8-2. Including the Script Reference in Your HTML Page

```
<!DOCTYPE html>
<html>
<head>
    <meta charset="utf-8" />
    <meta name="viewport" content="width=device-width">
    <title>MyFirstBlazor5</title>
    <base href="/" />
    <link href="css/bootstrap/bootstrap.min.css"
        rel="stylesheet" />
    <link href="css/site.css" rel="stylesheet" />
</head>
<body>
  <app>Loading...</app>

  <script src="_framework/blazor.webassembly.js"></script>
  <script src="scripts/interop.js"></script>
</body>
</html>
```

> When you use a Blazor component library you don't need to include the script in the index.html page. You will see an example of this later in this chapter.

Now let's look at how to call these setProperty/getProperty glue functions. Open the Index.cshtml Blazor component and modify it to look like Listing 8-3. To keep things simple, you will call the glue functions synchronously, which requires the IJSInProcessRuntime instance, which you will store in the IPR (in-process-runtime) variable.

Listing 8-3. Invoking the Glue Functions from a Blazor Component

```
@page "/"

<h1>Hello, world!</h1>

Welcome to your new app.

<input type="number" bind="@Counter" />

<SurveyPrompt Title="How is Blazor working for you?" />

@functions {

    private IJSInProcessRuntime IPR
    => (IJSInProcessRuntime)JSRuntime.Current;

    public int Counter
    {
      get
      {
        string value =
          IPR.Invoke<string>("interop.getProperty",
                            nameof(Counter));
        if( value != null && int.TryParse(value, out var v))
        {
          return v;
        }
        return 0;
      }
      set
      {
        IPR.Invoke<string>("interop.setProperty",
                            nameof(Counter), $"{value}");
      }
    }
}
```

This looks a bit like the Counter component, but now the Counter stores its value in the browser's window.localstorage. To do this you use a Counter property, which invokes your glue functions in the property setter and getter. These glue functions are synchronous, so you first create a private IPR property to store the IJSInProcessRuntime instance (because you don't want to repeat yourself, and copy-paste has been the cause of so many subtle bugs). Then in the Counter property's getter you invoke the window.interop.getProperty glue function. But because localstorage uses strings you need to convert between the Counter of type int and string. There's one more caveat: initially localstorage will not have a value yet, so if this returns a null reference you simply return 0. Similar in the Counter property's setter, you invoke the window.interop.setProperty glue function, making sure you convert the int to a string. This last conversion is quite essential; otherwise you will see errors in the browser's console.

Run the solution and modify the Counter's value. Now when you refresh your browser you will see the last value of Counter. The Counter is now persisted between sessions! You can exit your browser, open it again, and you will see the Counter again with the last value.

Passing a Reference to JavaScript

Sometimes your JavaScript needs to access one of your HTML elements. You can do this by storing the element in an ElementRef and then passing this ElementRef to the glue function.

Never use JavaScript interop to modify the DOM because this will interfere with the Blazor rendering process! If you need to modify the browser's DOM, use a Blazor component.

You should use this ElementRef as an opaque handle, meaning you can only pass it to a JavaScript glue function, which will receive it as a JavaScript reference to the element.

Let's look at an example by setting the focus on the Counter input element using interop. Start by adding a property of type ElementRef to the @functions area in Index.html as in Listing 8-4.

Listing 8-4. Adding an `ElementRef` Property

```
private ElementRef inputElement { get; set; }
```

Then modify the input element to set the `inputElement` property as in Listing 8-5.

Listing 8-5. Setting the `inputElement`

```
<input ref="@inputElement" type="number" bind="@Counter" />
```

Now add another glue function to `interop.js` as in Listing 8-6.

Listing 8-6. Adding the `setFocus` glue function

```
window.interop = {
  setProperty: function (name, value) {
    window.localStorage[name] = value;
    return value;
  },
  getProperty: function (name) {
    return window.localStorage[name];
  },
  setFocus: function (element) {
    element.focus();
  }
};
```

Now comes the "tricky" part. Blazor will create your component and then call the lifecycle methods such as `OnInit`. If you invoke the `setFocus` glue function in `OnInit` the DOM has not been updated with the input element so this will result in a runtime error because the glue function will receive a `null` reference. You need to wait for the DOM to be updated, which means that you should only pass the `ElementRef` to your glue function in the `OnAfterRender`/`OnAfterRenderAsync` method!

Add the `OnAfterRender` method to the `@functions` section as in Listing 8-7.

Listing 8-7. Passing the `ElementRef` in `OnAfterRender`

```
protected override void OnAfterRender()
{
  IPR.Invoke<string>("interop.setFocus", inputElement);
}
```

218

Run your solution and you should see that the input element receives focus automatically, as in Figure 8-1.

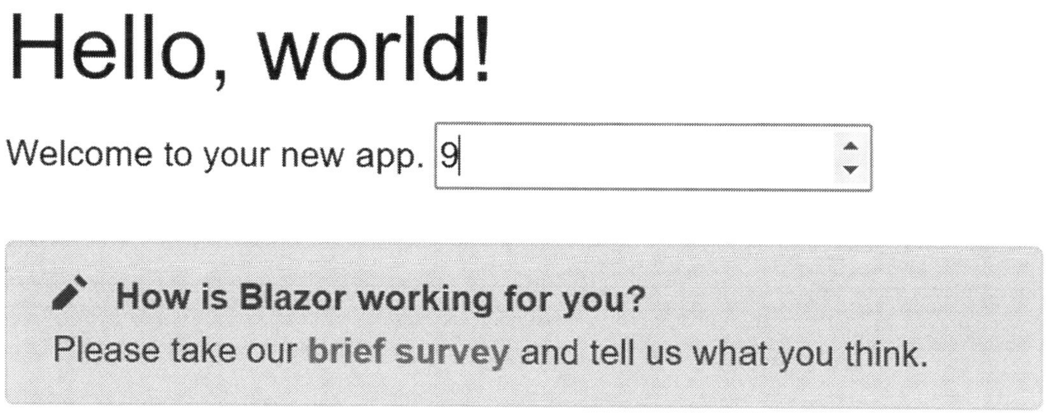

Hello, world!

Welcome to your new app. 9

✏ **How is Blazor working for you?**
Please take our **brief survey** and tell us what you think.

Figure 8-1. *The Counter receives focus automatically*

Calling .NET Methods from JavaScript

You can also call .NET methods from JavaScript. For example, your JavaScript might want to tell your component that something interesting has happened, like the user clicking something in the browser. Or your JavaScript might want to ask the Blazor component about some data it needs. You can call a .NET method, but with a couple of conditions. First, your .NET method's arguments and return value need to be JSON serializable, the method must be `public`, and you need to add the `JSInvokable` attribute to the method. The method can be a `static` or an instance method.

To invoke a static method, you use the JavaScript `DotNet.invokeMethodAsync` or `DotNet.invokeMethod` function, passing the name of the assembly, the name of the method, and its arguments. To call an instance method, you pass the instance wrapped as a `DotNetObjectRef` to a JavaScript glue function, which can then invoke the .NET method using the `DotNetObjectRef`'s `invokeMethodAsync` or `invokeMethod` function, passing the name of the .NET method and its arguments. Let's continue with the previous example. When you make a change to local storage, the storage triggers a JavaScript storage event, passing the old and new value (and more). This allows you to register for changes in other browser tabs or windows and use it to update the page.

Adding a Glue Function Taking a .NET Instance

Open interop.js from the previous example and add a watch function, as in Listing 8-8.

Listing 8-8. The watch Function Allows You to Register for Local Storage Changes

```
window.interop = {
  setProperty: function (name, value) {
    window.localStorage[name] = value;
    return value;
  },
  getProperty: function (name) {
    return window.localStorage[name];
  },
  setFocus: function (element) {
    element.focus();
  },
  watch: function (instance) {
    window.addEventListener('storage', function (e) {
      console.log('storage event');
      instance.invokeMethodAsync('UpdateCounter');
    });
  }
};
```

The watch function takes a reference to a DotNetObjectRef instance and invokes the UpdateCounter method when storage changes.

Adding a JSInvokable Method to Invoke

Open Index.cshtml and add the UpdateCounter method to the @functions area, as shown in Listing 8-9.

Listing 8-9. The UpdateCounter Method

```
[JSInvokable]
public Task UpdateCounter()
{
  this.StateHasChanged();
  return Task.CompletedTask;
}
```

This method triggers the UI to update with the latest value of Counter. Please note that this method follows the .NET async pattern returning a Task instance. Because you are not actually calling any async API, you return the Task.CompetedTask. To complete the example, add the OnInit lifecycle method shown in Listing 8-10.

Listing 8-10. The OnInit Method

```
protected override void OnInit()
{
  IPR.Invoke<string>("interop.watch",
                 new DotNetObjectRef(this));
}
```

The OnInit method wraps the Index component's this reference in a DotNetObjectRef and passes it to the interop.watch function.

To see this in action, open two browser tabs on your web site. When you change the value in one tab you should see the other tab update to the same value, as shown in Figure 8-2.

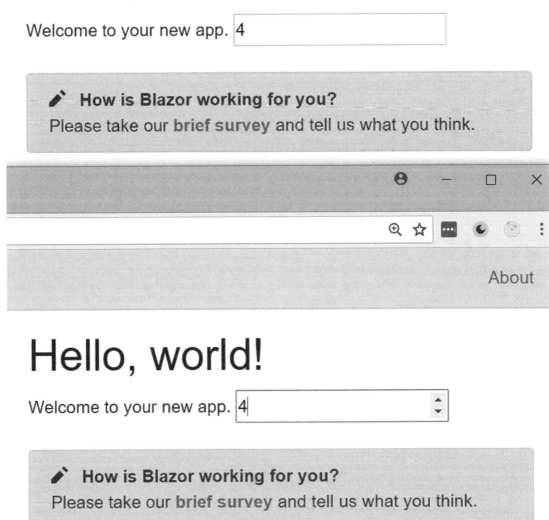

Figure 8-2. *Updating the Counter in one tab updates the other tab*

Building a Blazor Chart Component Library

In this section, you will build a *Blazor component library* to display charts by using a popular open source JavaScript library called Chart.js (www.chartjs.org). However, wrapping the whole library would make this chapter way too long, so you'll just use a simple line-chart component.

Creating the Blazor Component Library

Open Visual Studio and start by creating a new Blazor project called ChartTestProject, as shown in Figure 8-3. This project will only be used for testing the chart component.

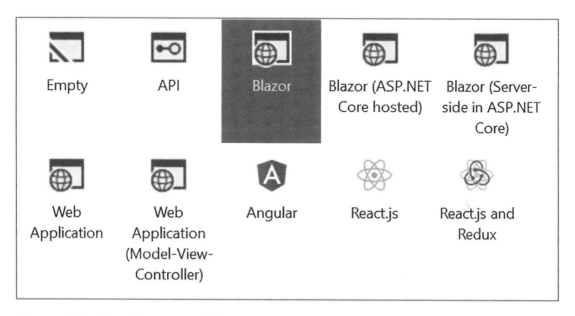

Figure 8-3. *Creating a new Blazor project*

If you are using Code, open a command prompt and type

```
dotnet new blazorhosted -o ChartTestProject
```

With both Visual Studio and Code, open a command prompt on the directory containing the ChartTestProject solution (the folder where the .sln file is) and type

```
dotnet new blazorlib -o U2U.Components.Chart
```

This will create a new *Blazor component library*. Unfortunately, you cannot create this kind of project with Visual Studio (yet). Go back to Visual Studio, right-click the solution, and select Add ➤ Existing Project. Select the U2U.Components.Chart project. Your solution should look like Figure 8-4.

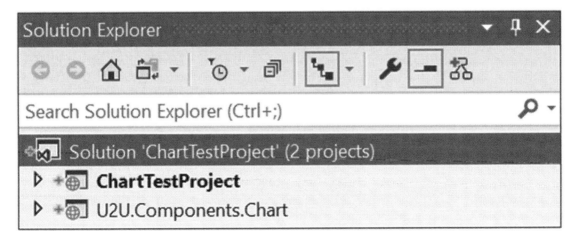

Figure 8-4. The solution containing the component library

If you're using Code, simply type this command to add the component library to the solution:

```
dotnet sln add U2U.Components.Chart/U2U.Components.Chart.csproj
```

Adding the Component Library to Your Project

Now you have the Blazor component library project. Let's use it in the test project. Look for Component1.cshtml in the U2U.Components.Chart project and rename it to LineChart.cshtml. Add a reference to the component library in the client project. In Visual Studio, right-click the ChartTestProject and select Add ➤ Reference. Check the U2U.Components.Chart project, shown in Figure 8-5, and click OK.

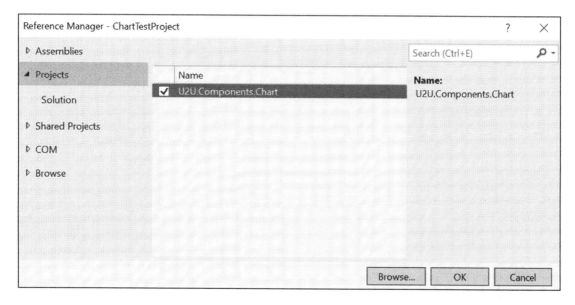

Figure 8-5. *Adding a reference to the component library*

With Code, use the integrated terminal, change the current directory to
ChartTestProject.Client, and type this command:

```
dotnet add reference ../U2U.Components.Chart/U2U.Components.Chart.csproj
```

This will add a reference to the U2U.Components.Chart component library.

Look for the _ViewImports.cshtml file (the one next to App.cshtml) in the
ChartTestProject and open it in the editor. Remember from Chapter 3 that to use
a component from a library you need to add it as an MVC tag helper. Insert the
@addTagHelper directive shown in Listing 8-11.

Listing 8-11. Adding the LineChart tagHelper to the Blazor Project

```
@using System.Net.Http
@using Microsoft.AspNetCore.Blazor.Layouts
@using Microsoft.AspNetCore.Blazor.Routing
@using Microsoft.JSInterop
@using ChartTestProject
@using ChartTestProjcct.Shared

@addTagHelper *, U2U.Components.Chart
```

Open the `Index.cshtml` file from the `Pages` folder and add the `LineChart` component shown in Listing 8-12.

Listing 8-12. Adding the `LineChart` Component

```
@page "/"

<h1>Hello, world!</h1>

Welcome to your new app.

<LineChart/>

<SurveyPrompt Title="How is Blazor working for you?" />
```

Build and run your application. It should look like Figure 8-6.

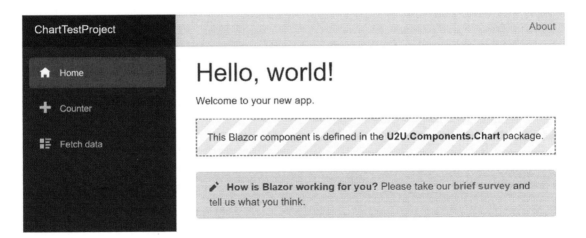

Figure 8-6. *Testing if the component library has been added correctly*

Adding Chart.js to the Component Library

The `LineChart` component doesn't look like a chart, so it's time to fix this! First, you need to add the `Chart.js` JavaScript library to the component library project. Go to `www.chartjs.org/`. This is the main page for `Chart.js`. Now click the GitHub button, shown in Figure 8-7, to open the project's GitHub page.

Chart.js

Simple yet flexible JavaScript charting for designers & developers

Figure 8-7.   *The Chart.js main page*

Scroll down this page looking for the GitHub releases link. Press this link with your mouse and the release page will open, as shown in Figure 8-8.

Since it takes some time between writing a book and you reading it there is a big chance that the version will have incremented. Make sure you select a version starting with 2, since version 3 will contain breaking changes.

Click Chart.bundle.min.js to download it, as shown in Figure 8-8.

Latest release

v2.7.2

98f104c

Version 2.7.2

chartjs-ci released this on Mar 1 · 0 commits to release since this release

Assets

Chart.bundle.js	523 KB
Chart.bundle.min.js	206 KB
Chart.js	394 KB
Chart.js.zip	393 KB
Chart.min.js	156 KB
Source code (zip)	
Source code (tar.gz)	

Figure 8-8. *GitHub releases page for Chart.js*

After it has been downloaded, copy this file to the content folder of the U2U.Components.Chart project, as shown in Figure 8-9. All files in this folder are automatically downloaded into the browser by Blazor so you don't need to add them to index.html.

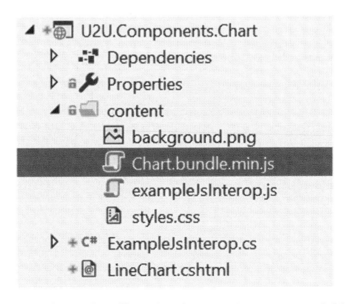

Figure 8-9. *Copying* Chart.bundle.min.js *into the contents folder*

Verifying If the JavaScript Library Loaded Correctly

You know about Murphy's Law? It states, "Anything that can possibly go wrong, does." Let's make sure that the Chart.js library gets loaded by the browser. Run your Blazor project and open the browser's debugger. Check if Chart.bundle.min.js has been loaded correctly. The easiest way to do this is to see if window.Chart has been set (Chart.js adds one constructor function called Chart to the window global object). You can do this from the Console tab of the debugger by typing window.Chart, as shown in Figure 8-10.

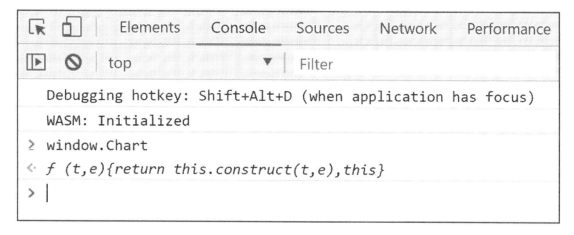

Figure 8-10. *Using the browser's console to check the value of* window.Chart

If this returns undefined, rebuild the U2U.Components.Chart project. Then you can try refreshing the browser after emptying the browser's cache. When the browser's debugger is shown, right-click the refresh button and you'll get a drop-down menu, as shown in Figure 8-11. Select the Empty Cache and Hard Reload menu item.

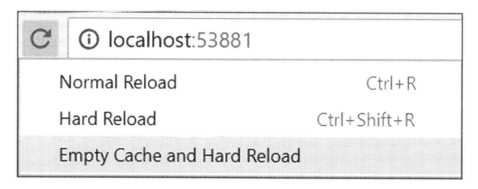

Figure 8-11. *Reloading the page after clearing the cache*

Adding Chart.js Data and Options Classes

Open your browser and type in www.chartjs.org/docs/latest/. Here you can see a sample of using Chart.js in JavaScript. This library requires two data structures to be passed to it: one containing the chart data and one containing the options. This section will add these classes to the Blazor component library, but now using C#. Again, I am not going for full coverage of all the features of Chart.js to keep things crisp.

The ChartOptions Class

Let's start with the options class. Right-click the U2U.Components.Chart library and add a new class called ChartOptions as in Listing 8-13.

This is a fair amount of code. You might consider copying it from the sources provided with this book. I've also left out comments describing each property for conciseness.

Listing 8-13. The ChartOptions Class

```
public class ChartOptions
{
  public class TitleOptions
  {
    public static readonly TitleOptions Default
    = new TitleOptions();

    public bool Display { get; set; } = false;
  }
  public class ScalesOptions
  {
    public static readonly ScalesOptions Default
    = new ScalesOptions();

    public class ScaleOptions
    {
```

```csharp
    public static readonly ScaleOptions Default
    = new ScaleOptions();

    public class TickOptions
    {
      public static readonly TickOptions Default
      = new TickOptions();

      public bool BeginAtZero { get; set; } = true;

      public int Max { get; set; } = 100;
    }

    public bool Display { get; set; } = true;

    public TickOptions Ticks { get; set; }
    = TickOptions.Default;
  }

  public ScaleOptions[] YAxes { get; set; }
  = new ScaleOptions[] { ScaleOptions.Default };
}

public static readonly ChartOptions Default
= new ChartOptions { };

public TitleOptions Title { get; set; }
= TitleOptions.Default;

public bool Responsive { get; set; } = true;

public bool MaintainAspectRatio { get; set; } = true;

public ScalesOptions Scales { get; set; }
= ScalesOptions.Default;
}
```

This C# class, with nested classes, reflects the JavaScript options object (partially) from Chart.js. Note that I've added Default static properties to each class to make it easier for developers to construct the options hierarchy.

The LineChartData Class

Chart.js expects you to give it the data it will render. For this, it needs to know a couple of things, like the color of the line, the color of the fill beneath the line, and, of course, the numbers to plot the graph. So how will you represent colors and points in your Blazor component? As it turns out, there are classes in .NET to represent colors and points: System.Drawing.Color and System.Drawing.Point. Unfortunately, you cannot use Color because it doesn't convert into a JavaScript color, but you can allow users to use it in their code. I'll discuss how to do this a little later. Add a new class LineChartData to the component library called LineChartData, as shown in Listing 8-14.

Listing 8-14. The LineChartData Class

```
using System;
using System.Collections.Generic;
using System.Drawing;

namespace U2U.Components.Chart
{
  public class LineChartData
  {
    public class DataSet
    {
      public string Label { get; set; }

      public List<Point> Data { get; set; } = null;

      public string BackgroundColor { get; set; }

      public string BorderColor { get; set; }

      public int BorderWidth { get; set; } = 2;
    }

    public string[] Labels { get; set; }
    = Array.Empty<string>();

    public DataSet[] Datasets { get; set; }
  }
}
```

Most of this class should be clear, except maybe for `Array.Empty<string>()`. This method returns an empty array of the generic argument. But why is this better? You cannot modify an empty array, so you can use the same instance everywhere (this is also known as the *Flyweight Pattern*). This is like `string.Empty` and using it puts less strain on the garbage collector.

Registering the JavaScript Glue Function

To invoke the `Chart.js` library you need to add a little JavaScript of your own. Open the `content` folder of the component library project and start by renaming the `exampleJsInterop.js` file to `JsInterop.js` and replacing the code with Listing 8-15.

Listing 8-15. Registering the JavaScript Glue Class

```
window.components = (function () {
  return {
    chart: function (id, data, options) {
      var context = document.getElementById(id)
                          .getContext('2d');
      var chart = new Chart(context, {
        type: 'line',
        data: data,
        options: options
      });
    }
  };
})();
```

This adds a `window.components.chart` glue function that when invoked calls the `Chart` function (from `Chart.js`), passing in the graphics `context` for the canvas, `data`, and `options`. It is very important that you pass the `id` of the canvas because someone might want to use the `LineChart` component several times in the same page. By using a unique id for each `LineChart` component you end up with canvasses with unique ids.

233

Providing the JavaScript Interoperability Service

Your LineChart component will need to call the Chart.js library using your window.components.chart glue function. But putting all this logic in the LineChart component directly is something you want to avoid. Instead, you will build a service encapsulating this logic and inject the service into the LineChart component. Should the Blazor team at Microsoft decide to change the way JavaScript interoperability works (they have done that before) then you will only need to change one class (again, the *Single Responsibility Principle*). Start by adding a new interface to the U2U.Components.Chart library project called IChartInterop with the code from Listing 8-16.

Listing 8-16. The IChartInterop Interface

```
namespace U2U.Components.Chart
{
  public interface IChartInterop
  {
    void CreateLineChart(string id, LineChartData data,
                                   ChartOptions options);
  }
}
```

As you can see, this interface's CreateLineChart method closely matches the window.components.chart glue function. Let's implement this service. Add a new class called ChartInterop to the component library project and implement is as in Listing 8-17.

Listing 8-17. Implementing the ChartInterop Class

```
using Microsoft.JSInterop;

namespace U2U.Components.Chart
{
  /// <summary>
  /// It is always a good idea to hide specific implementation
  /// details behind a service class
  /// </summary>
  public class ChartInterop : IChartInterop
```

234

```
{
  public void CreateLineChart(string id, LineChartData data,
                              ChartOptions options)
  {
    JSRuntime.Current
            .InvokeAsync<string>("components.chart",
                                  id, data, options);
  }
}
}
```

This `CreateLineChart` method invokes the JavaScript `components.chart` function you added in Listing 8-15.

Time to configure dependency injection. You could ask the user of the library to add the `IChartInterop` dependency directly, but you don't want to put too much responsibility in the user's hands. Instead you will provide the user with a handy *C# extension method* that hides all the gory details from the user. Add the new class called `DependencyInjection` to the component library project with the code from Listing 8-18.

Listing 8-18. The `AddCharts` Extension Method

```
using Microsoft.Extensions.DependencyInjection;

namespace U2U.Components.Chart
{
  public static class DependencyInjection
  {
    public static IServiceCollection AddCharts(
      this IServiceCollection services)
    => services.AddSingleton<IChartInterop, ChartInterop>();
  }
}
```

This class provides you with the `AddCharts` extension method that the user of the `LineChart` component can now add to the client project. Let's do this. Make sure everything builds first, and then open `Startup.cs` in the `ChartTestProject` and add a call to `AddCharts` as in Listing 8-19.

Listing 8-19. Convenient Dependency Injection with `AddCharts`

```
using Microsoft.AspNetCore.Blazor.Builder;
using Microsoft.Extensions.DependencyInjection;
using U2U.Components.Chart;

namespace ChartTestProject
{
  public class Startup
  {
    public void ConfigureServices(IServiceCollection services)
    {
      services.AddCharts();
    }

    public void Configure(IBlazorApplicationBuilder app)
    {
      app.AddComponent<App>("app");
    }
  }
}
```

The user of the component does not need to know any implementation details to use the LineChart component. Mission accomplished!

Implementing the LineChart Component

Now you are ready to implement the LineChart component. Chart.js does all its drawing using an HTML5 canvas element, and this will be the markup of the LineChart component. Update LineChart.cshtml to match Listing 8-20.

Listing 8-20. The LineChart Component

```
@inject IChartInterop JsInterop

<canvas id="@Id" class="@Class">
</canvas>
```

```
@functions {

  [Parameter]
  protected string Id { get; set; }

  [Parameter]
  protected string Class { get; set; }

  [Parameter]
  LineChartData Data { get; set; }

  [Parameter]
  ChartOptions Options { get; set; } = ChartOptions.Default;

  protected override void OnAfterRender()
  {
    string id = Id;
    JsInterop.CreateLineChart(Id, Data, Options);
  }
}
```

The LineChart component has a couple of parameters. The Id parameter is used to give each LineChart's canvas a unique identifier; this way you can use LineChart several times in the same page. The Class parameter can be used to give the canvas one or more CSS classes to add some style (and you can never have enough style). Finally, the Data and Options parameters get passed to JavaScript to configure the chart.

Now comes the tricky part (this is like the earlier section where you wanted to set the focus on the input). To call the JavaScript chart function, the canvas needs to be in the browser's DOM. When does that happen? Blazor creates the component hierarchy, calls each component's OnInit, OnInitAsync, OnParameterSet, and OnParameterSetAsync methods, and then uses the component hierarchy to build its internal tree, which then is used to update the browser's DOM. Then Blazor calls each component's OnAfterRender and OnAfterRenderAsync methods. Because the canvas element should already be part of the DOM you need to wait for the OnAfterRender method before calling JsInterop.CreateLineChart.

Using the LineChart Component

With everything in place, you can now complete the LineChart component from the Index page in your ChartTestProject. Update the Index.cshtml file to match Listing 8-21. You will add the toJS() extension method later, so ignore any errors till then.

Listing 8-21. Completing the Index Component

```
@page "/"
@using U2U.Components.Chart
@using System.Drawing

<h1>Hello, world!</h1>

Welcome to your new app.

<LineChart Id="test" Class="linechart"
          Data="@Data" Options="@Options" />

<SurveyPrompt Title="How is Blazor working for you?" />

@functions {

private LineChartData Data { get; set; }

private ChartOptions Options { get; set; }

protected override void OnInit()
{
  this.Options = ChartOptions.Default;

  this.Data = new LineChartData
  {
    Labels = new string[] { "", "A", "B", "C" },
    Datasets = new LineChartData.DataSet[]
    {
      new LineChartData.DataSet
      {
        Label = "Test",
        BackgroundColor = Color.Transparent.ToJs(),
        BorderColor =  Color.FromArgb(10, 96, 157, 219)
                           .ToJs(),
```

```
        BorderWidth = 5,
        Data = new List<Point>
        {
          new Point(0,0),
          new Point(1, 11),
          new Point(2, 76),
          new Point(3,13)
        }
      }
    }
  };
}
}
```

You start by adding two @using directives for the U2U.Components.Chart and System. Drawing namespaces. Then you add the Id, Class, Data, and Options parameters. You give these parameters values in the OnInit method (should you get this data from the server you would use the OnInitAsync method). One more thing before you can build and run the project and admire your work: add a new class called ColorExtensions to the U2U. Component.Chart project. Implement it as shown in Listing 8-22.

Listing 8-22. The ColorExtensions Class with the toJS Extension Method

```
using System.Drawing;

namespace U2U.Components.Chart
{
  public static class ColorExtensions
  {
    public static string ToJs(this Color c)
    => $"rgba({c.R}, {c.G}, {c.B}, {c.A})";
  }
}
```

Build and run your project. If all is well, you should see Figure 8-12.

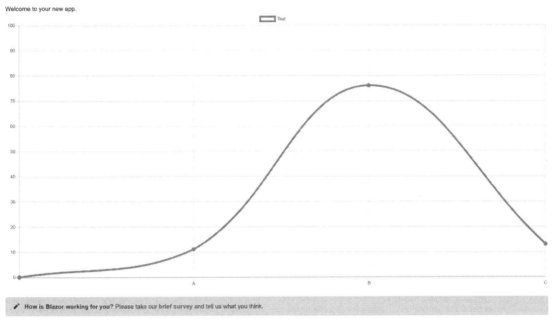

Figure 8-12. The finished chart example

Summary

In this chapter, you saw how you can call JavaScript from your Blazor components using the `JSRuntime.Current.InvokeAsync<T>` method. This requires you to register a JavaScript glue function by adding this function to the browser's window global object.

You can also call your .NET static or instance method from JavaScript. Start by adding the `JSInvokable` attribute to the .NET method. If the method is static, you use the JavaScript `DotNet.invokeMethodAsync` function (or `DotNet.invokeMethod` if the call is synchronous), passing the name of the assembly, the name of the method, and its arguments. If the method is an instance method, you pass the .NET instance wrapped in a `DotNetObjectRef` to the glue function, which can then use the `invokeMethodAsync` function to call the method, passing the name of the method and its arguments.

Finally, you applied this knowledge by wrapping the `Chart.js` open source library to draw a nice line chart. You built *a Blazor component library*, added some classes to pass the data to the `Chart` function, and then used a glue function to draw the chart.

Index

© Peter Himschoot 2019
P. Himschoot, *Blazor Revealed*, https://doi.org/10.1007/978-1-4842-4343-5

Static page, 187
System.ValueTuple NuGet package, 39

T

ToggleAlert method, 58
TransferService, 112
Transient dependencies, 111
Two-Way Data Binding
    date format, 26
    syntax, 24–26

U

Universal Resource Identifiers (URI)
        and verbs, 126
UseBlazor method, 132

UseResponseCompression
    Middleware, 12
U2U.Components.Chart project, 229

V

Visual Studio generation
    dotnet cli generation, 7, 8
    project creation, 6, 7
    running
        counter page, 9
        Fetch data tab, 9, 10
        home page, 8

W, X, Y, Z

WeatherForecast class, 163

—